ME AND MY WORLD

By Lynn Cohen
Illustrated by Susan Pinkerton

ABOUT THE AUTHOR

Lynn Cohen received her B.S. in education from S.U.N.Y. at New Paltz, and M.S. in remedial reading from Johns Hopkins University. Education of children, teachers, college students, and parents has been her main focus for fourteen years. She teaches early childhood and elementary education at S.U.N.Y College at Farmingdale and S.U.N.Y. College at Old Westbury and is an early childhood consultant.

Publisher: Roberta Suid
Editor: Bonnie Bernstein
Cover Design: David Hale
Design and Production: Susan Pinkerton
Cover art: Corbin Hillam

Monday Morning is a registered trademark
of Monday Morning Books, Inc.

ISBN 0-912107-46-4

Printed in the United States of America

9 8 7 6 5 4 3 2 1

CONTENTS

INTRODUCTION

Familiar faces and familiar routines characterize the everyday world of toddlers and two-year-olds. Children at this age are full of their own self-importance, and enjoy knowing just how the world will revolve around them from waking till bedtime. Dressing, eating, napping, playing, shopping—these predictable activities give young children a sense of security.

Me and My World takes the reassuring themes of early childhood and integrates them in a lively play curriculum of reading, art, music, and movement activities for children ages 15 months to three years. These ideas are appropriate for the home, nursery schools, day care centers, libraries, "Mommy and Me" programs, and the like.

For toddlers and twos, learning is all child's play—hours of make-believe, experimenting with messy materials, collecting and classifying toys, running and climbing and jumping. These activities foster new language and social skills, and help small children develop muscular coordination.

Me and My World features practical yet appealing activities that spin off on children's natural play. The necessary materials and props are those you'd ordinarily find around the home or in the nursery crafts closet. Projects and games have all been home and classroom tested.

To begin a new theme or unit, read aloud books from the list of recommendations. You can find most selections at your local library. Follow up with an art project, then a song or movement activity. Continue the unit a day or a week, as your time and your children's interests dictate. Use as many ideas as you like, including your own. Drop an idea that doesn't hold the children's interest; come up with variations to extend an activity they really enjoy.

Art activities usually involve some preassembly by an adult ("precuts"), a little demonstration, then the children take over. Interfere as little as possible; there is no "right way" to do things. If you give a child a chunk of carrot for stamping, don't correct her technique if she prefers to drag it over the paper like a paintbrush. Expect a toddler or two-year-old to paint or paste only one or two objects rather than fill the page, and to make designs or squiggles rather than something you might recognize. Only children at the upper end of this age range will even attempt a representative drawing or painting.

Filling the page, using the right technique, keeping tidy—these are unimportant. What is important is that your children feel free to express themselves however they like, experiment with whatever materials you can provide, and learn from the delightful mess they are making. At the very least, they are developing hand-eye coordination.

The verbal abilities of toddlers and twos vary considerably. Sing songs even if the children can't sing along. Instead, encourage them to listen and perform creative movements along with you. Young children can communicate their understanding in ways other than words; meanwhile, they are picking up language as they listen.

Take a similar thematic approach in designing your own integrated unit or program. Choose art techniques that your children can manage, and have them use these techniques on precut shapes or preassembled forms. Change familiar song lyrics spontaneously so you and your children can sing about what they are doing, or wearing, or wondering about. Use pantomime and movement to give the children a creative outlet for their often boundless energy.

Chapter One:

All About Me

cut out paper eyeglasses

→

have children cut out and paste paper eyes on their eyeglasses

MY BODY

We marvel at the tiny but perfect features of infants, and watch with tender amusement as their little limbs respond reflexively to our touch. But before long, babies' features grow, their limbs lengthen, and they become energetic children developing control of their small bodies. Now it's time to show toddlers and two-year-olds how to identify their own body parts.

ART ACTIVITIES

EYEFUL OF EYEGLASSES

Materials: Construction paper, scissors, old magazines, paste.
Preparation: Cut out paper eyeglasses. Also cut out pairs of eyes from old magazine pictures.
Activity: Children paste eyes in the eyeglasses.

BLUE EYES? BROWN EYES?

Materials: Mirror, white construction paper, cotton swabs, paint.
Preparation: Children look at their eyes in the mirror. Identify each child's eye color.
Activity: Children use cotton swabs to paint the color of their eyes—brown, green, black, or blue—on white construction paper.

BIG MOUTH

Materials: Red construction paper, scissors, old magazines, glue.
Preparation: Cut a big mouth out of the red paper. Cut pictures of mouths out of magazines.
Activity: Children glue little mouths on a big mouth.

SOFT HAIR

Materials: Mirror, construction paper, yarn to match hair colors, glue.
Preparation: Children look at the color of their hair in the mirror. Identify each child's hair color. Cut out different lengths of yarn—yellow, brown, black, and orange—to match hair colors.
Activity: Children match their hair color with the appropriate color yarn. They paste that color yarn on construction paper.

HAND AND FOOT PRINTS

Materials: Construction paper, paint, styrofoam meat tray or shallow pan, bucket of water, soap, towel.
Preparation: Pour paint in the styrofoam tray or pan.
Activity: Children place a hand or foot flat in the tray of paint, then print with it on paper. Help the children wash up immediately.

FEELY PICTURES

Materials: Construction paper, feathers, sand paper, steel wool pads, felt scraps, velour or velvet scraps, cotton, glue.
Activity: Children glue materials of various textures on construction paper. They feel the different textures with their hands. Then they close their eyes, touch, and guess what kind of material they're feeling.

I'M A BOY. I'M A GIRL.

Materials: Sponge, scissors, snap clothespins, construction paper, styrofoam meat tray, paint.
Preparation: From the sponge, cut out conventional figures of a boy and girl. Clip a clothespin onto the sponge cutouts. Pour paint in the styrofoam tray.
Activity: Children use a boy or girl sponge, the same sex as themselves, to sponge paint a figure on the construction paper.

MUSIC AND MOVEMENT ACTIVITIES

PIGGY TOES

Partners take off their shoes and touch toes with each other, then take turns playing "This Little Piggy." One player says the nursery rhyme while giving each toe on the other player's foot a little shake, beginning with the big toe and working down to the little toe.

> This little piggy went to market.
> This little piggy stayed home.
> This little piggy had roast beef.
> This little piggy had none.
> And this little piggy cried
> "Whee-whee-whee-whee-whee!"
> All the way home.

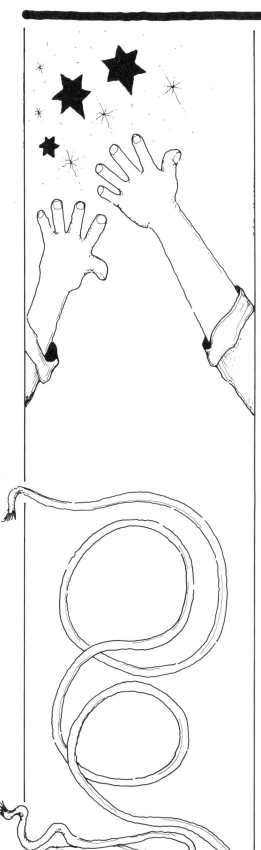

BODY PART EXERCISES

Children become more aware of their bodies and learn to identify the different body parts by exercising them.

Head: Move heads left and right, saying "No!" while moving. Move heads up and down, saying "Yes!" while moving.

Arms and Hands: Shake arms and hands like "wet spaghetti." Reach for stars, first with the right hand, then the left. When stars are caught, put them in pockets. Make an elephant's trunk—bend at the waist, clasp hands, swing arms back and forth.

Back: Children press the soles of their feet together, touch their foreheads to their toes, rounding their backs.

Legs and Feet: Pretend the legs are bicycles. Children lie on their backs and kick their legs in the air. Pretend the legs are butterflies. Children sit up straight, press the soles of their feet together, and flap their knees up and down.

ROPE WALKING

Spread a long rope or thick cord over a large area, making several loops. Children walk the rope barefooted, following it from one end to the other. Reposition the rope to play again.

SONG: "Head and Shoulders, Knees and Toes"

Children touch corresponding body parts as they sing this song to the tune of "London Bridge Is Falling Down."

Head and shoulders, knees and toes,
Knees and toes, knees and toes.
Head and shoulders, knees and toes,
Eyes, ears, mouth, and nose.

GROWING UP

Children pretend to be babies and act out your suggestions. First the babies sleep. Then they open their eyes. Mothers are rocking the babies. Babies roll over on their tummies, then crawl, then stand up and walk. Now baby isn't a little baby anymore. "Now (name of child) is two (or however many) years old!"

MY CLOTHING

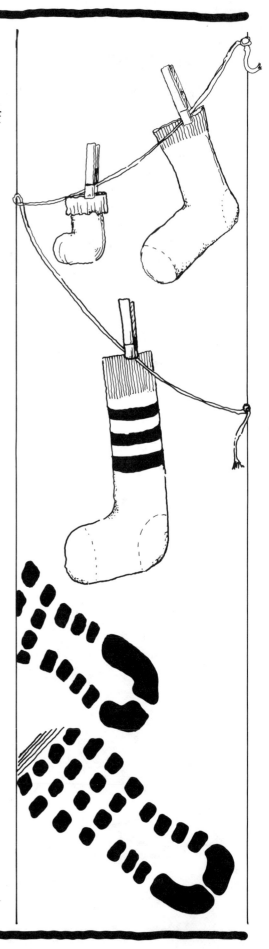

Getting dressed is part of every child's morning routine. What do we wear each day? Help children name the kinds of clothes they wear. How do your clothes look and feel? Talk about colors and textures. Compare a soft white undershirt to a stiff new pair of blue jeans. Help children observe the sizes and shapes of different articles of clothing—how knee socks are longer than ankle socks, and how a glove accommodates five fingers but a mitten has only a thumb. Talking to children while dressing, changing, or toileting them is a marvelous way to develop their language, visual discrimination, understanding of spatial relationships, and sensory perception.

ART ACTIVITIES

LOTS OF SOCKS

Materials: Wide assortment of socks, fabric scraps, scissors, construction paper, glue.
Preparation: Cut different-sized sock shapes out of fabric scraps—Mommy's socks, baby's socks, etc.
Activity: Show children the assorted socks. Discuss the differences in color, texture, and size. Use the words *big* and *little* as you show toddlers a big and little sock. Let older two-year-olds help you sequence the socks from smallest to largest.

Give the children sock cutouts to glue on construction paper in size sequence or in relative groups of big and little socks (a simpler task).

SHOELACE PAINTING

Materials: Construction paper, styrofoam meat tray, paint, shoelace.
Preparation: Pour paint in the styrofoam tray.
Activity: Children hold one end of a shoelace and dip the other end in the paint. They drag the lace across the paper to paint.

SHOE PRINTS

Materials: Old or outgrown shoes or boots, styrofoam meat tray, paint, oaktag.
Preparation: Pour paint in the styrofoam tray.

staple
cut out
socks
together

have children hold
pipe cleaners and
decorate their socks

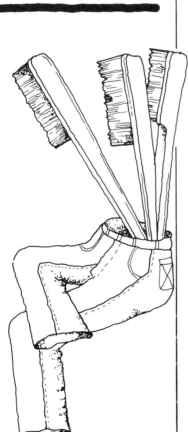

Activity: Children place a shoe or boot in the tray of paint, then print with it on the oaktag. Sneakers with waffle soles or other patterned soles make especially good prints.

SUPER SOCK

Materials: Brown wrapping paper or paper bag, scissors, stapler, pipe cleaners, styrofoam meat tray, paint, old newspapers.

Preparation: Cut a very large sock shape out of the brown paper. Use the shape as a pattern to cut out another. Staple the socks together along the edges, leaving an opening at the heel. Bend one end of each pipe cleaner into a different shape, twisting the other end into a handle as shown. Pour paint in the styrofoam tray.

Activity: Children dip the pipe cleaners into the paint and print designs on their socks. When both sides are painted and dry, the children crumple newspapers into small wads and help you stuff the insides of their socks. Staple closed the heels.

FEELY CLOTHING COLLAGE

Materials: Yarn, different-textured fabric scraps (cotton, velvet, velour, vinyl, feathers, leather, fur), scissors, oaktag, glue.

Preparation: Cut yarn and assorted fabric scraps into small pieces.

Activity: Children glue fabric scraps on oaktag. Discuss what kinds of clothing are made from the different-textured pieces (shoes from leather, etc.).

MY SHIRT AND PANTS

Materials: Construction paper, scissors, buttons, fabric scraps, glue.

Preparation: Cut shirt and pants shapes out of paper.

Activity: Children glue buttons on their shirts and fabric on their pants.

BLUE JEANS

Materials: Pairs of blue jeans from various family members, construction paper, scissors, styrofoam meat tray, blue paint, toothbrush.

Preparation: Cut pants shapes out of construction paper. Pour paint in the styrofoam tray.

Activity: Show children the different pairs of jeans—Dad's long jeans, big sister's jeans with stitched pockets, the children's own small jeans. Give each child a paper pants cutout and a toothbrush. Children dip their toothbrushes in the paint and paint their jeans blue.

BUTTON MY OVERALLS

Materials: Construction paper, scissors, outgrown jeans, buttons, glue.
Preparation: Cut an overalls shape out of construction paper. Cut up one or more pairs of outgrown jeans into small swatches.
Activity: Children glue buttons on the straps of their overalls, then glue on denim swatches as decoration.

PAINT ON A SMOCK

Materials: Newsprint or wallpaper sample book (paint stores are usually willing to give away outdated books), scissors, smock, easel, large jar of paint, large paintbrush.
Preparation: Cut a large smock shirt shape out of newsprint or wallpaper sample page and attach it to an easel. If an easel is unavailable, work on the floor, protecting the area with newspaper. Help the children put on their smocks.
Activity: Discuss how smocks protect clothes. Children use large muscles to paint their paper smocks.

WOOLLY CLOTHES

Materials: Construction paper, scissors, yarn, glue.
Preparation: Cut mitten, scarf, and sweater shapes out of paper. Snip yarn into small pieces.
Activity: Children glue yarn on the paper cutouts.

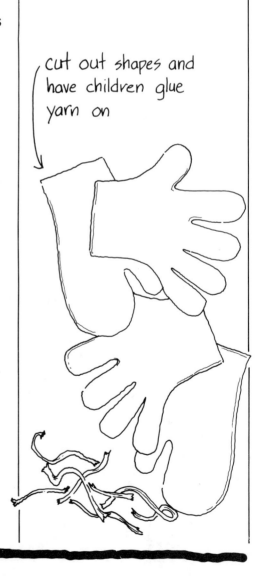

cut out shapes and have children glue yarn on

MUSIC AND MOVEMENT ACTIVITIES

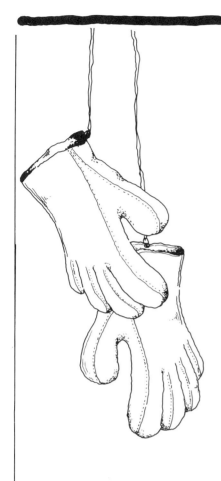

WHERE IS THUMBKIN?

Props: Gloves and mittens.
Activity: Wearing gloves, play and sing "Where Is Thumbkin?", repeating for ring finger, middle man, pointer, and pinky. Wearing mittens, just perform the first verse.

> Where is thumbkin? Where is thumbkin? (*Hide hands behind back.*)
> Here I am. (*Bring out right thumb.*) Here I am. (*Bring out left thumb.*)
> How are you today, sir? (*Wiggle right thumb to make it "talk."*)
> Very well I thank you. (*Make left thumb "talk."*)
> Run and play. (*Exit right hand again.*) Run and play. (*Exit left hand again.*)

THREE LITTLE KITTENS LOST THEIR MITTENS

Record the sound of kittens crying (real kittens or someone pretending). Provide pairs of mittens and a pie tin. Have the children wear mittens as they recite the nursery rhyme, "Three Little Kittens," and mime the action.

> Three little kittens lost their mittens
> (*Show mittens, then make them disappear.*)
> And they began to cry,
> (*Play tape as children pretend to weep.*)
> "Oh, Mother dear, we greatly fear
> That we have lost our mittens!"
> "Lost your mittens! You naughty kittens!
> Now you shall have no pie!"
> (*Show pie tin and shake finger angrily.*)

ZIPPETY, ZIP! STAND STILL!

Children follow your directions to move about until you hold up a large zipper and call, "Zippety, zip!" (You might find it easier to interrupt your own prerecorded directions if a tape player is available.) Movements might include "Walk, walk, walk around the room," "Hop, hop, and flop like a bunny," "Run, run, run as fast as you can or I'll catch you and gobble you up!"

SONG: "Karen's Wearing a Red Dress"

If possible, read *Mary Wore Her Red Dress and Henry Wore His Green Sneakers* by Merle Peek. Then sing this song to the tune of "Johnny Plays with One Hammer." Repeat often, substituting the names of the children and the kinds of clothing they are wearing.

> Karen's wearing a red dress,
> A red dress, a red dress.
> Karen's wearing a red dress
> All day long.

GETTING DRESSED IN THE MORNING

Children do a pantomime of their daily dressing routine as you narrate: "First Mommy (or Daddy, or name some other caregiver) puts on your diaper or underpants. Undershirt goes over the head. Right arm through the sleeve, then left. Help Mommy put on your shirt. Right arm, left arm. Button the buttons—one, two, three, four." Continue with socks, then pants or overalls, zipping the zippers. Last on are the sneakers—tie the laces or snap the velcro fastener.

MY FAMILY AND FRIENDS

A toddler and two-year-old's world centers around the family—grandparents, parents, brothers and sisters, new babies. These are the people who love, nurture, and give children a sense of security. From the experience of being loved, children learn to love in return, and before long their affections grow to include little friends among the important people in their lives. Activities that center around family and friends are sure to absorb and delight them.

ART ACTIVITIES

I LOVE MY FAMILY

Materials: Red or pink construction paper, scissors, old magazines, glue.
Preparation: Cut a large heart out of construction paper. Also cut out pictures of people and families from magazines. Include grandparents.
Activity: Talk about the children's families. You may need to say that some children have only one parent, that some have brothers and sisters while others are "only" children, or that some have a grandparent living with them. Then the children glue magazine cutouts on the paper hearts.

DADDY'S SHAVING CREAM PAINTING

Materials: Finger paint paper or butcher paper, shaving cream, food coloring.
Preparation: Squirt shaving cream on paper. Add a few drops of food coloring.
Activity: Children finger paint with the shaving cream. *Note: If you don't want stained fingers, leave out the food coloring; it doesn't wash off.*

MOMMY'S POCKETBOOK

Materials: Construction paper, old magazines, scissors, glue.
Preparation: Fold construction paper in half. Cut out a pocketbook shape along the fold. Also cut pictures of items you'd find in a pocketbook out of old magazines (e.g., wallet, make-up, tissues, keys, comb).
Activity: Children "open" their pocketbooks and glue cutout items inside.

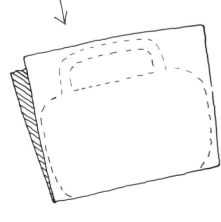

fold construction paper in half and cut out pocketbook

MOMMY'S ROLLERS

Materials: Construction paper, plastic hair rollers, styrofoam meat tray, paint.
Preparation: Pour paint in the styrofoam tray.
Activity: Children dip the rollers into the paint, then paint or print designs on paper. They might also try stamping circles with the open ends, or making patterned tracks by rolling the roller back and forth.

BROTHER AND SISTER STENCILS

Materials: Oaktag, scissors, construction paper, masking tape, one-inch-thick paintbrush, paint.
Preparation: Cut stencils of a conventionalized little girl and boy out of oaktag. Tape the stencil on top of the construction paper.
Activity: Children paint through the appropriate stencil for each brother and sister in their families. Move the stencil to other parts of the paper to make the necessary number. Write the names of brothers and sisters under the pictures that represent them. Children who have no brothers or sisters can use the stencils to paint boy and girl cousins or friends.

FRAME FOR A FAMILY FRIEND

Materials: Oaktag, scissors, crayons, photo of family or a friend, glue, adhesive picture hook (optional).
Preparation: Fold the oaktag and cut out a large rectangle along the fold. Unfold the rectangle. Cut out a window in one half, about a half-inch shorter in both dimensions than the photo.
Activity: Children draw on their frames, then glue the photo face forward behind the window. Stand the frame by positioning the open ends a little apart, or glue an adhesive picture hook on the back and hang.

MUSIC AND MOVEMENT ACTIVITIES

FINGER PLAY: "Where's My Family?"

Sing this song to the tune of "Where Is Thumbkin?", introducing a different finger from behind your back for each verse to represent that member of the family. You can also use the names of children in a playgroup.

fold and glue photo behind window

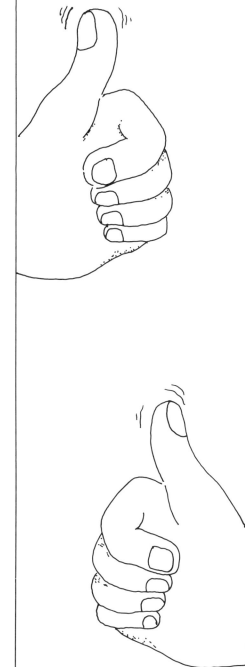

Where is Daddy? Where is Daddy?
Here I am. Here I am. (*Bring righthand thumb from behind your back, then lefthand thumb.*)
How are you today, Dad? (*Wiggle one thumb to make it talk.*)
Very well I thank you! (*Wiggle other thumb.*)
Go back home! Go back home! (*Exit one thumb, then the other, behind back.*)

Repeat, singing "Where is Mommy? Where is sister? Where is brother? Where is baby?", bringing out a new finger each time. Then sing "Where's the whole family?", bringing out a handful of fingers.

WHO AM I?

Children improvise with only a thick yarn hair ribbon to show characteristics of the members of their families. For example, the children can position ribbons on their faces to make Daddy's mustache or beard, on their heads to show Mommy's long hair, or looped on an ear to show her earring. A shake of the ribbon might suggest a baby brother's rattle; a turn of the ribbon, big sister's bike. *Note: Children two-and-a-half years old won't need suggestions; they can come up with their own improvisations.*

DADDY SHAVING

The children pretend to be daddies shaving. First they wet their faces, then they squirt shaving cream on their hands and rub it all over their cheeks and necks. Now they take their razors and shave off those whiskers!

MY HOME

Whether it is an apartment or house, large or small, in a city or the country—a young child's home is a very special place. The home environment is where children first learn to label objects and to take apart and put back together familiar things. They sense order and notice change. Most important, home is where children first learn about security and safety.

ART ACTIVITIES

MURAL HOUSE

Materials: Wallpaper sample book, scissors, old department store catalogs, glue.

Preparation: Cut out the shape of a large house or apartment from a wallpaper sample page. Cut pictures of furniture and large household appliances out of the catalogs. Include pictures of architectural features, such as windows, doors, and fireplaces.

Activity: Children glue the picture cutouts in the house or apartment. Two-year-olds can first sort pictures according to what room they would appear in—bedroom, bathroom, living room, kitchen. Draw lines to divide the house or apartment into four rooms so the children can glue appropriate cutouts in each room.

TURN ON THE OVEN

Materials: Construction paper, styrofoam meat tray, paint, sponge, snap clothespin, bottle caps, glue.

Preparation: Cut the shape of a stove-top oven out of paper. Attach a piece of sponge to a clothespin. Pour paint in the styrofoam tray.

Activity: Children glue on bottle caps for stove and oven knobs, then sponge paint their stove-top ovens.

HOUSE PAINTING

Materials: Pail of water, large paintbrush, large sponge.
Activity: Children go outdoors to water-paint the outside walls of the house or a fence using brushes and sponges.

have children glue cutouts on house cutout

staple plastic wrap to frame

attach art behind frame and lift curtain to view

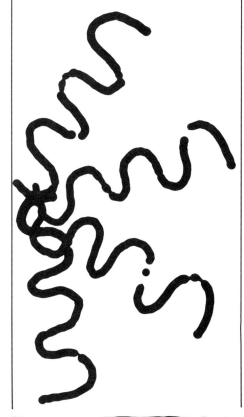

WINDOW CURTAINS

Materials: Oaktag, plastic wrap, stapler and staples, fabric pieces, construction paper, crayons.
Preparation: Cut a window frame out of oaktag. Staple plastic wrap on the back of the frame. Staple fabric pieces on front of the frame for curtains.
Activity: Children color on paper (suggest they draw an "outside" picture). Glue their drawings behind the window frames. Children lift the curtains and see their art in the window.

WHAT'S IN THE REFRIGERATOR?

Materials: White construction paper, old magazines, glue.
Preparation: Cut a refrigerator shape out of paper. Cut pictures of food items out of magazines.
Activity: Children glue food cutouts on their refrigerators.

EASEL HOUSE PAINTING

Materials: Newsprint, scissors, easel, newspaper, paint, brushes.
Preparation: Cut a large shape of a house or apartment building out of the newsprint. Attach it to an easel. Protect the floor with newspaper.
Activity: Children paint their houses.

UTENSIL PRINTING

Materials: Kitchen utensils (such as forks, spoons, potato masher, cups, spatula, meat tenderizer, grater), paper, styrofoam meat tray, paint.
Preparation: Pour paint in the styrofoam tray.
Activity: Children dip utensils in the paint, then print with them. *Note: This activity is recommended for older two-year-olds.*

MY PLACE AT THE TABLE

Materials: Construction paper, paper napkin, plastic fork and spoon, paper plate and cup, glue.
Activity: Children use paper as placemats. They set their own place by gluing on a plate, cup, and napkin, then gluing the fork and spoon on top of the napkin.

MUSIC AND MOVEMENT ACTIVITIES

NOISES IN MY HOUSE

Find pictures of the following noisemakers, or the objects themselves: telephone, vacuum, alarm clock, smoke alarm, dishwasher, people, sink, television, radio, teapot. Show the children the picture or object as you name it and reproduce its sound (the actual sound, or your own voice approximation). Ask the children to reproduce the sounds with their own voices.

HOOPS IN THE HOUSE

The children use hoops as props to act out your suggestions. Ask for their own ideas as well and have the children act them out.

   Washing machines: Children swirl hoops around their waists, pretending to be washing machine agitators. They can chant, "Wash, wash, wash your clothes, wash your clothes clean!"
   Windows: Children peer through their hoops as if they are windows. They move them up and down to open and close the windows.
   Doors: Children step through their hoops as if they are doors to a room in the house.
   Vacuum cleaner: Children hold hoops in front of themselves, with the far end touching the floor. They make the sound of a vacuum while pushing the hoops along the floor.

CLOCKS

Show the children a picture of a clock with a pendulum. The children swing their arms like a pendulum as they sing or recite the nursery rhyme, "Hickory, Dickory, Dock."

Chapter Two:

When I'm Home

MY MEALS

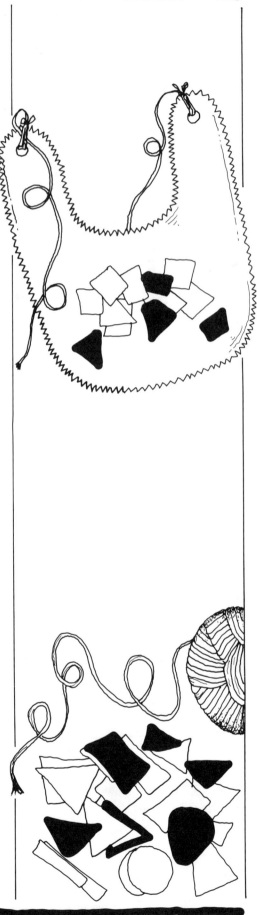

Mealtime gives children an opportunity to learn about their senses. They taste their food, smell it cooking, observe the many colors, and feel the various textures and consistencies. They giggle when they hear themselves crunch into crisp vegetables and listen thirstily as the juice is poured. Amid all this stimulation, hungry toddlers confined in highchairs are often still struggling to pick up their meals with a spoon, while two-year-olds perched on booster seats are busy negotiating with a fork. Make the most of their interest and efforts at mealtime by introducing new foods and talking about how and what the children are going to eat.

ART ACTIVITIES

MY BEAUTIFUL BIB

Materials: Construction paper, scissors or pinking shears, hole punch, yarn, tissue paper, glue.
Preparation: Cut a bib shape out of paper. (Pinking shears will produce a decorative edge.) Punch a hole at the top of each side. Attach yarn in the holes for ties. Cut the tissue paper into small pieces.
Activity: Children glue tissue paper on their bibs as decoration. Maybe they'd like to wear their bibs at snack time.

BOWLS OF CEREAL OR COTTAGE CHEESE

Materials: Construction paper, scissors, glue, Cheerios or styrofoam packaging peanuts.
Preparation: Cut a bowl shape out of paper.
Activity: The Cheerios or styrofoam peanuts represent cottage cheese. The children glue them on their bowls.

FORK PRINTING

Materials: Different-sized forks (baby fork, dinner fork, barbeque fork), paper, styrofoam meat tray, paint.
Preparation: Pour a small amount of paint in the styrofoam tray.
Activity: Children press the forks in the paint, then print with them on paper.

FRIED EGGS WITH KETCHUP

Materials: White and yellow construction paper, red paint, squeeze bottle, glue.

Preparation: Cut out a white paper oval to represent the egg white and a smaller yellow paper circle to represent the yolk. Fill the squeeze bottle with red paint.

Activity: Make fried eggs for breakfast. After breakfast, the children make their own eggs by gluing the paper yolks on the paper whites, then squeezing red paint on top to represent ketchup.

EGG SHELL MOSAIC

Materials: Eggshells, food coloring, rubbing alcohol, white construction paper, scissors, glue.

Preparation: Save eggshells. Wash them and let them dry out for a few days, then break them into tiny pieces. Dye the pieces in a mixture of food coloring and alcohol, then let them dry. Cut large ovals out of the white paper to represent eggs.

Activity: Children glue the dyed eggshells on a paper egg.

PEANUT BUTTER SANDWICHES

Materials: Brown construction paper, scissors, peanut shells, glue.

Preparation: Cut out a brown paper square. Draw a line down the middle of the square to divide the "sandwich" into halves.

Activity: Children glue cracked peanut shells onto their sandwiches. *Note: You can process the unused peanuts in an electric blender or food processor to make peanut butter for real sandwiches.*

BOLOGNA SANDWICHES

Materials: Styrofoam meat trays, scissors, pink construction paper, brown marker, glue, paper plate.

Preparation: Cut out two same-size squares of styrofoam for the bread slices. Draw along the outer edges with the brown marker to make the "crust." Cut a circle out of the pink construction paper for bologna (make the diameter slightly larger than the width of the square).

Activity: Children glue the bologna circle in between the styrofoam bread slices, then glue the whole sandwich onto a paper plate.

have children glue cracked shells onto their sandwiches

CUPS OF MILK

Materials: Colored construction paper, scissors, styrofoam meat tray, white paint, toothbrush.
Preparation: Cut the shape of a training cup with handles out of construction paper. Pour the paint in the styrofoam tray.
Activity: Children use toothbrushes to paint milk in their cups.

VEGETABLE AND FRUIT STAMPS

Materials: White construction paper, scissors, green crayon or marker, styrofoam meat trays, paint, carrots, potatoes, apples.
Preparation: Cut the shapes of a carrot, potato, and apple out of the white paper. Color the stems of the apple and carrot green. Pour orange, brown, and red paint in the styrofoam trays. Cut the carrot, potato, and apple in half widthwise.
Activity: Children press the vegetable or fruit into the appropriate color paint, then stamp or paint on the corresponding construction paper shape. *Note: Do only one vegetable or fruit in a day.*

MY FAVORITE FOODS

Materials: Old magazines, scissors, paper plates, glue.
Preparation: From the magazines, cut out pictures of healthy foods your children like to eat.
Activity: Children glue food cutouts on paper plates.

PUDDING PAINTING

Materials: Instant pudding, washable surface (such as vinyl placemat, plastic tray, or formica table).
Preparation: Prepare the pudding mix according to the directions.
Activity: Children finger paint with pudding on a washable surface, licking their fingers as much as they like.

CHOCOLATE CHIP COOKIES

Materials: Brown grocery bag, scissors, styrofoam meat tray, brown paint.
Preparation: Cut a cookie shape out of the brown paper bag. Pour the paint in the styrofoam tray.
Activity: Children dip their thumbs in the paint then make thumb print chocolate chips on their paper cookies.

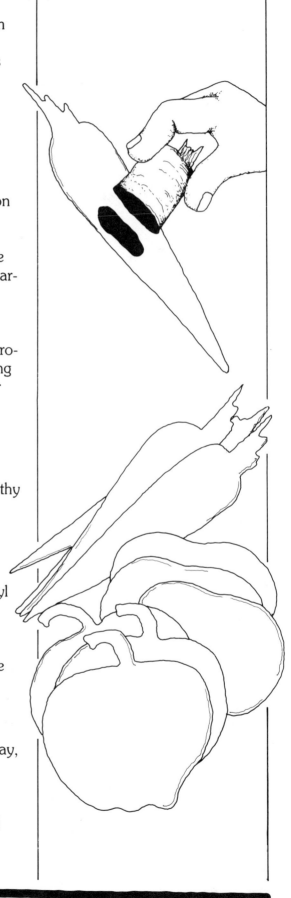

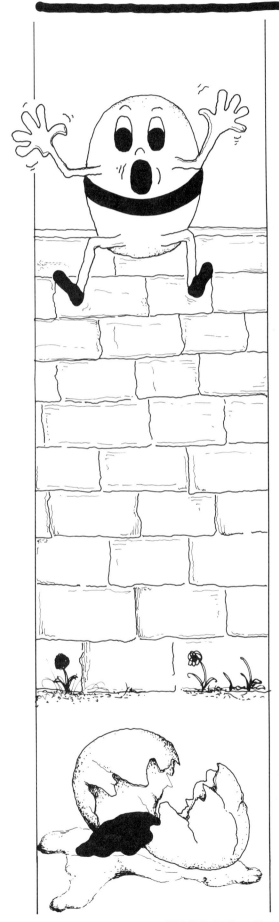

MOSAIC FISH

Materials: Paper plate, scissors, stapler, marker, different-colored tissue papers, glue.

Preparation: Cut a wedge out of one edge of the plate and staple it onto the opposite edge to make a fish. Draw in an eye with the marker. Cut or tear the tissue paper into small pieces (about an inch square).

Activity: Children paste tissue paper scales on the paper plate fish.

MUSIC AND MOVEMENT ACTIVITIES

HUMPTY DUMPTY

Show the children an egg and a picture of Humpty Dumpty. Explain that Humpty Dumpty is only an egg. Drop the real egg in a bowl so the children can see why Humpty Dumpty can't be put back together again. Recite and act out the nursery rhyme together.

> Humpty Dumpty sat on a wall. (*Sit on a table.*)
> Humpty Dumpty had a great fall. (*Fall down.*)
> All the King's horses (*Gallop and neigh.*)
> And all the King's men (*March like soldiers.*)
> Couldn't put Humpty together again.

SCRAMBLING EGGS

Children pretend to make breakfast. Suggest these actions: Take out a bowl. Crack the eggs against the rim of the bowl. Beat the eggs. Pour them into a pan. Stir the eggs. Put the eggs on a plate and eat them. After cooking and eating, pretend to wash and dry the dishes.

PRETZELS

Sit with the children in a circle on the floor. Show them how to fit the soles of their feet together, then have them move their legs up and down so they flap like butterflies. Next touch your toes to your mouth so that your body assumes a pretzel-like position. Tell the children to taste their own salty pretzels.

LET'S MAKE HOT CEREAL

For this recipe, actions are the ingredients.

Pour salt and water in a pot and boil.
(*Children jump up and down.*)
Pour oatmeal into the pot and stir.
(*Children run around in a circle.*)
Pour the cereal in a bowl. It's hot!
(*Children blow on imaginary bowls.*)
Pour milk on the oatmeal to cool it down. Now it's just
right! (*Children pretend to pour, then taste.*)

PAT-A-CAKE

Sing and clap out this nursery rhyme substituting your children's names.

Pat-a-cake, pat-a-cake, baker's man.
Bake me a cake as fast as you can.
Roll it up (*Roll hands.*)
And pat it (*Pat hands.*)
And mark it with a *T*. (*Draw imaginary letter in the air.*)
Put it in the oven for Teddy and me!

SONG: "Eating My Dinner"

Sing this song to the tune of "Here We Go Round the Mulberry Bush" and have the children pantomime.

This is the way I eat my dinner
Eat my dinner, eat my dinner.
This is the way I eat my dinner
When I am very hungry.

Other verses:

This is the way I feed myself. . .(*Pretend to bring spoon to mouth.*)
This is the way I chew my meat. . .(*Chew.*)
This is the way I drink my milk. . . (*Drink.*)
I swallow all my vegetables. . . (*Swallow.*)
Mom's happy when I eat all up. . . (*Smile.*)

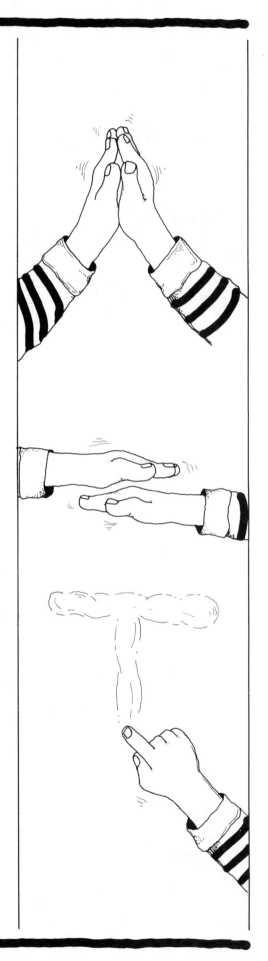

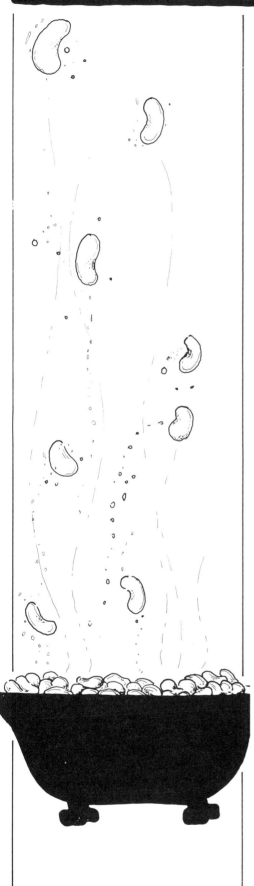

MY BATH AND POTTY

The success of a small child's day is usually directly proportional to the mess on hands, face, and clothing. A bath is essential whether children love or dislike the water. You can help reluctant bathers overcome their fear and dislike for the water by setting up water play activities. Fill the bathtub or classroom water table with dolls, meat basters, eye droppers, toy dishes, boats, squeeze bottles, funnels, and plastic containers. As they dip, pour, and splash, children have fun and learn at the same time.

The bathroom is also host to a near future activity—toileting. Although children ages 18 to 24 months may be introduced to the toilet, research indicates they will not master toilet training until about 2½ years. Usually boys take longer to acquire the physiological control than girls. Hurrying children before they are physically and psychologically ready can upset and frustrate both children and adults. But once children understand about toileting, you can encourage them with a few related art activities and simple songs included in this section.

ART ACTIVITIES

BUBBLE BATH

Materials: Blue construction paper, scissors, styrofoam packaging peanuts, glue.
Preparation: Cut a bathtub shape out of the blue paper.
Activity: Children glue styrofoam peanuts on the bathtub cutout to represent bubbles.

SOAP PAINTING

Materials: Dark colored construction paper, soap flakes (for example, Ivory Snow), water, bowl, measuring cup, eggbeater or electric beater.
Preparation: Pour two cups of soap flakes and ½ cup of water into the bowl. Beat until the soap mixture has the consistency of thick whipped cream.
Activity: Children finger paint with the soap mixture on dark colored paper.

MY BATH TOWEL

Materials: White construction paper, scissors, terry cloth (old washcloths or towels will do), glue.
Preparation: Fringe the edges of the white paper to look like a fringed towel. (Some two-year-olds can do this themselves.) Cut old terry cloths or towels into small pieces.
Activity: Children glue the terry scraps on their paper towels.

TOWEL BLOTS

Materials: Square of terry cloth, cotton balls, rubber band, paint, styrofoam meat tray, paper.
Preparation: Place several cotton balls in the center of the terry cloth. Draw up the sides and fasten with a rubber band. Pour the paint in the styrofoam tray.
Activity: Children dab the stuffed terry cloth square in the paint, then make blots on their papers.

TOOTH AND NAIL BRUSH PAINTING

Materials: Toothbrushes, nail brushes, paint, styrofoam meat tray, paper.
Preparation: Pour paint in the styrofoam tray.
Activity: Children paint with toothbrushes and nail brushes on paper.

SWIM LIKE A DUCK

Materials: Rubber duck bath toy, yellow construction paper, scissors, yellow feathers (available in small bags at craft supplies stores), glue.
Preparation: Cut a duck shape out of yellow paper.
Activity: Show the children the rubber duck. Ask who likes to swim and splash like a duck in the bath. Hand out the duck cutouts and feathers. Children glue feathers on their ducks.

SPONGE THROW MURAL

Materials: Brown wrapping paper or old sheet, sponges, styrofoam meat trays, paints, smocks or old shirts.
Preparation: Tape the paper or sheet on the floor. Pour paint in the styrofoam trays. Help the children put on their smocks or shirts.
Activity: Children dip sponges in paint and throw them onto the "mural." Then they pick them up, dip, and toss again.

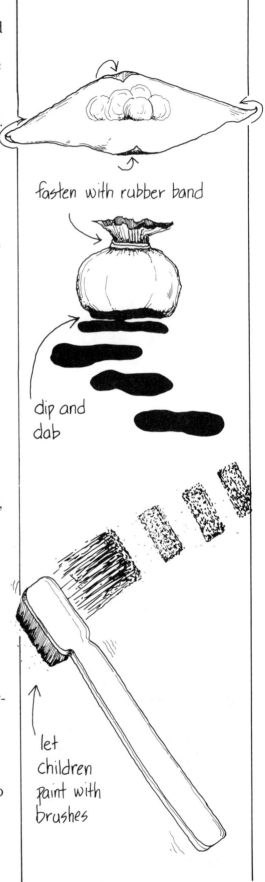

fasten with rubber band

dip and dab

let children paint with brushes

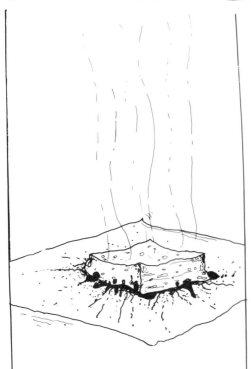

TOILET TUBE PRINTS

Materials: Empty toilet paper tubes, styrofoam meat tray, paint, construction paper.
Preparation: Pour paint in the styrofoam tray.
Activity: Children dip one end of the toilet tube in paint, then print circles on paper.

TOILET PAPER COLLAGE

Materials: Dark colored construction paper, toilet paper in a variety of pastel colors, stick glue.
Activity: Children tear the toilet paper into small pieces, then glue them on the construction paper.

I WEAR UNDERPANTS

Materials: Construction paper, scissors, glue.
Preparation: Cut out a paper doll or draw a picture of a small person. The doll or person should have your child's name on it. Cut out a pair of underpants to fit the figure.
Activity: Children glue underpants on their dolls.

MOVEMENT ACTIVITIES

WET SPONGES

Ask the children to pretend to be sponges. Have them follow your suggestions for acting out: "Lie down in a big bathtub of water. (*Children lie on floor.*) The sponge fills up with water. (*Children stand up and round their arms to show swelling.*) Now Mom comes along and squeezes you. (*Children hug themselves, or another child, or Mom.*) Water drips from you. (*Children put their arms over their heads and drop to the floor.*) Pitter patter go the water drops as they splash into a puddle on the floor!" (*Children repeat the "pitter patter" sound.*)

ROWBOATS

Partners pretend to be rowboats. They sit facing one another on the floor with their legs outstretched and their heels touching one another's. The partners hold hands and rock back and forth as they sing "Row, Row, Row Your Boat."

let children glue on underpants on their paper dolls

BUBBLE CHASE

You'll need some bubble solution and a wand. Blow bubbles as the children chase them. Have them blow bubbles themselves, pretending to be the wind, as you hold the wand. Can they catch a bubble? Stamp it out? Hop on a bubble? Float with it?

MY BATH SONG

Teach the children this song to the tune of "Twinkle, Twinkle Little Star."

See me washing in the tub
Look at all the parts I scrub
First my eyes and ears and nose
Then my fingers and my toes
My tummy and my bottom, see
I'm clean and shiny as can be!

MY BATHTUB

A large refrigerator box makes a great make-believe bathtub (ask a local appliance store to save one for you). A few children go into the box and pretend to take a bath. First they wash all their body parts with soap. Next they shampoo their hair and let Mom rinse out the soap. Then they play, kicking and splashing as they pretend to swim. When it's time to get out, hand the children imaginary towels so they can dry themselves off. Now they're nice and clean!

SONG: "Flush, Flush, Flush the Potty"

Sing this song to the tune of "Ten Little Indians." You can substitute *toilet* for *potty* if that is the word your children use.

Flush, flush, flush the potty
Flush, flush, flush the potty
Flush, flush, flush the potty
(child's name) is a big *(boy or girl)*!

MY NAP AND BEDTIME

When bright eyes become tired eyes, it's time to go to sleep. Simplify bedtime and naptime for children by establishing a routine. Toddlers and two-year-olds need a transitional activity to relax and reassure them before settling into their cribs or beds. Sing lullabies or recite nursery rhymes, read aloud stories, or cuddle in a rocking chair. When the children are awake, remind them of the more comforting aspects of sleep with some related activities.

ART ACTIVITIES

PATCHWORK QUILT

Materials: Squares of calico fabric (about 6 inches square), buttons, felt scraps, cotton, sequins, bric-a-brac, white glue, large sheet of oaktag, stapler.
Activity: Children glue buttons and other decorations on calico squares. Staple the squares on the sheet of oaktag to make a large quilt.

MY PILLOW

Materials: Heavy white construction paper, scissors, stapler, white feathers, cotton, glue, newspaper.
Preparation: Staple two pieces of construction paper together, leaving one side open.
Activity: Children glue feathers and cotton on their pillows. When the glue has dried, the children help stuff the pillow with crumpled pieces of newspaper. Staple the open end closed.

FEATHER PAINTING

Materials: Feather, white construction paper, styrofoam meat tray, paint.
Preparation: Pour paint in the styrofoam tray.
Activity: Explain that some pillows are stuffed with feathers and let the children feel a down pillow if you have one. The children dip a feather in the paint and paint a paper pillow.

NIGHT SKY

Materials: Dark blue and white construction paper, styrofoam packaging stars, scissors, glue.

staple 2 pieces of paper together leaving one end open for stuffing

let children glue feathers and cotton on their pillows

stuff and staple closed

Preparation: Cut star and moon shapes out of white construction paper.

Activity: Take your children outdoors at night to look at the moon and stars. The next day, the children glue the star and moon cutouts and the styrofoam stars on dark blue paper to make their own night skies.

MY CRIB OR BED

Materials: Finger paint paper or shelf paper, scissors, finger paint.

Preparation: Cut the shape of a crib or bed out of finger paint paper or shelf paper.

Activity: Children finger paint their paper beds using the same color as their own real spreads or blankets.

MY PAJAMAS

Materials: Construction paper, scissors, flannel scraps, glue.

Preparation: Cut shirt and pants shapes out of construction paper. If the nights are cold, one-piece pajamas with feet may be a more appropriate cutout.

Activity: Children glue flannel on their pajamas.

MY SLIPPERS

Materials: Construction paper, scissors, fur scraps.

Preparation: Cut a slipper shape out of the paper.

Activity: Children glue fur on their slippers.

MUSIC AND MOVEMENT ACTIVITIES

REACH FOR THE STARS

Children bend, then straighten and stretch their arms over their heads to reach for a star. They pretend to put the star in their pockets. Repeat these movements, singing "Twinkle, Twinkle, Little Star."

SLEEPYTIME

The children act out their bedtime routines as you give directions: "Take off your clothes. Wash your hands and face. Brush your teeth. Sit down and help put on your pajamas. Brush your hair. Climb into your bed (or crib) and put your head on your pillow. Let me tuck you in. Lights out! Goodnight!"

let children glue fur pieces on their slippers

have children paint their shoeboxes

attach shoelace to decorated shoebox

MY TOYS

How do you direct the energy of toddlers or two-year-olds? Let them play with toys. Playtime is a very constructive outlet; as children play, they learn. As they make their dolls and stuffed animals talk, they are enhancing their own language skills and practicing socialization. They can act out behaviors and emotions through play that are unacceptable in other situations. Toys such as play dough or pegboards help children release energy and aggression while they're being creative and having fun.

ART ACTIVITIES

BALL PAINTING

Materials: Shoebox, construction paper, scissors, paint, small ball.
Preparation: Cut the construction paper to the dimensions of the bottom of the shoebox and lay it inside. Pour a few spoonfuls of paint onto the paper. Place the ball in the box.
Activity: Children hold the shoebox in their hands and tilt it to make the ball roll back and forth through the paint. The rolling ball will track paint, leaving an interesting design on the paper,

PULL TOY

Materials: Shoebox, hole punch, paint, paintbrush, shellac or acrylic sealer, shoelaces.
Preparation: Punch a hole in one short end of the shoebox.
Activity: Children paint their shoeboxes. When the boxes are dry, spray them with acrylic sealer or paint over them with clear shellac to help preserve them. Then tie long shoelaces through the holes. *Note: Some toddlers won't paint the entire shoebox in one sitting. Extend the project over a few days if necessary.*

WHEELS ON THE CAR

Materials: Construction paper, scissors, wagon wheel macaroni, glue.
Preparation: Cut a car shape out of construction paper.
Activity: Children glue macaroni wheels on their cars.

BLOCK PRINTING

Materials: Set of small cube blocks with letters or pictures carved on all sides (although any blocks will do), styrofoam meat tray, paint, paper.
Preparation: Pour the paint in the styrofoam tray.
Activity: Children press one face of the block at a time into the paint, then onto their papers to make prints.

SO MANY DOLLS!

Materials: White construction paper, scissors, watercolor paints, small paintbrushes, water.
Preparation: Fold the construction paper over four or five times. Cut out a doll figure, extending the arms from one fold to the other so the multiple dolls will all be holding hands when you unfold them. Wet the doll chain with a paintbrush and water. (Toddlers won't always remember to wet their brushes before painting with watercolors, so this measure will keep the paper moist enough to spread the paint.)
Activity: Children paint their paper dolls with watercolors.

DUM-DEE-DUM DRUM

Materials: Empty coffee can, solid color contact paper (self-adhesive), pencil, masking tape, tubes of acrylic paint.
Preparation: Cover the sides of the coffee can with contact paper. Wrap both ends of the pencil with several layers of masking tape.
Activity: Children squeeze acrylic paint around the sides of the coffee can to make a design. When the paint dries, they can beat their drums with their pencil drumsticks.

MY BABY DOLL

Materials: Brown wrapping paper or paper bag, scissors, stapler, fabric scraps, glue, old newspapers, infant-size paper diaper (optional).
Preparation: Fold the brown paper in half to cut out the front and back of a baby doll figure. Staple the front and back together along the edges, leaving a three-inch opening for stuffing. Use a dark-colored marker to outline a T-shirt and bottoms on the doll (bottoms unnecessary if you have a paper diaper).
Activity: Children help draw the doll's features (tell you where to draw the eyes, nose, etc., if they can't do it themselves), then decorate the doll's clothing with markers. Show them how to diaper their babies.

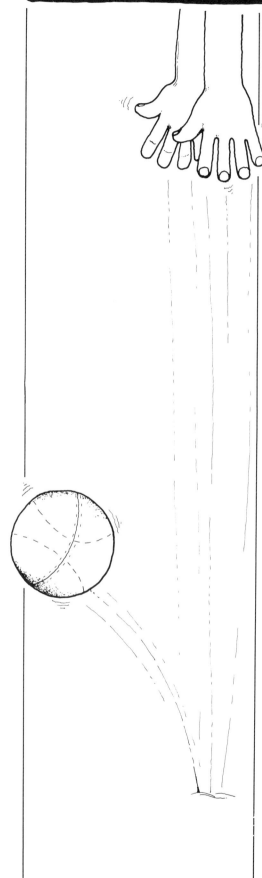

MUSIC AND MOVEMENT ACTIVITIES

SONG: "Here's a Ball for Baby"

As the children recite or sing this nursery rhyme, they use their hands to show the actions.

Here's a ball for baby
Big and soft and round. (*Hands curve to show ball.*)
Here is baby's hammer
See how baby pounds. (*Make a fist and move arm up and down.*)
Here are baby's hands
Clapping music so. (*Clap hands.*)
This is the way that baby says
Peek-a-boo! (*Cover and uncover eyes.*)

ROLLING BALLS

Children sit in a circle with their legs outstretched. They roll a large ball to each other as they chant this jingle:

Roll that big ball down to town
Roll that big ball down to town
Roll that big ball down to town
Down to town it goes.

The ball can go other places, too—down the hill, to the store, in the box, etc.

BOUNCING BODY BALLS

Children pretend to be balls. They lie on the floor out-stretched, first rolling forward, then backward. With your assistance, they roll in complete circles. Then the children become bouncing balls as they stand and jump up and down. They take turns throwing balls by gently pushing one child into the arms of another, who "catches" the ball with a hug before throwing it to the next child.

SLEEPY BABY DOLLS

Two children, or you and one child, hold a large towel open by the corners and rock a baby doll in the middle as you sing "Rock-a-bye Baby."

Rock-a-bye baby
On the tree top.
When the wind blows
The cradle will rock.
When the bough breaks
The cradle will fall;
Down will come baby,
Cradle and all. (*Drop ends of towel.*)

MARCHING DRUMS

Play some marching music on a record or cassette player. Children play drums and other rhythm instruments as they march around the room to the music.

GOING FOR A DRIVE

Children pretend to drive an imaginary car. They get in, shut the door, buckle their seat belts and turn the key in the ignition. As the car starts, they steer the wheel. Direct them in traffic: "Stop for the stop sign! Foot on the break! Okay, go again. Oh, no! It's starting to rain! Turn on your windshield wipers. Slow down. Turn your wheel. You're back on the road to your home. Park your car. Unbuckle your seat belt. Now get out. Don't forget your keys! Home at last!"

CAR WHEELS

Children get into their cars by stepping into hoops and holding them at their waists. They make car motor sounds as they drive their cars around the room. Change the activity a little by suggesting that the children hold their hoops in front of them like steering wheels.

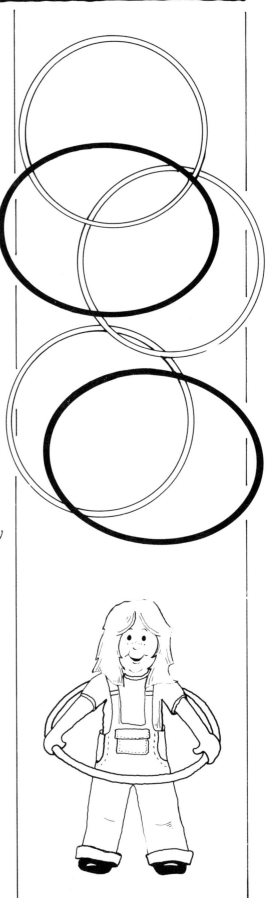

Chapter Three:

When I'm Out

MY YARD

By eighteen months, toddlers have mastered the skill of walking and are ready for a new world of gross motor play. Most indoor space suddenly seems inadequate for their energetic activities. It's time to open doors to the outside world. First stop—the backyard, where toddlers and two-year-olds explore new space and discover a bit of nature.

ART ACTIVITIES

HAIRY PEOPLE

Materials: Small plastic flower pot, plastic eyes with moving eyeballs (sold in fabric or craft supplies stores), buttons, red pipe cleaner, glue, potting soil, grass seed, pitcher of water.
Activity: Children help glue on moving eyeballs or button eyes, a button nose, and a pipe cleaner mouth on the flower pot. When the glue is dry, the children put handfuls of soil into the pot until it is half full. They sprinkle grass seed on top, fill the rest of the pot with soil, then water the seeds. Place the pot in a warm, light place. Within a week, the pot person will have grown hair!

MY LAWN MOWER

Materials: Construction paper, scissors, black marker, fake grass (the kind you put in Easter baskets), glue.
Preparation: Cut the shape of a lawn mower out of construction paper. Outline the edge with the marker.
Activity: Children glue fake grass on their mowers.

VEGETABLE GARDEN PRINTS

Materials: Brown construction paper, roll of green crepe paper, scissors, glue, potato, onion, carrot, styrofoam meat trays, paint (brown, yellow, and orange).
Preparation: Glue a strip of crepe paper for grass on the short ends of the construction paper garden. Cut the vegetables in half crosswise. Pour the paints in the trays.
Activity: Children dip the vegetables in the appropriate color paint and print a garden full of potatoes, onions, and carrots on the brown paper.

PAPER PLATE FLOWERS

Materials: Solid color paper plate, scissors, green construction paper, stapler, colored paper scraps, glue.

have children decorate their pots

add soil, seeds, soil, and water

Voila! Hair within a week!

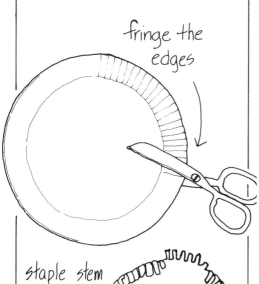

fringe the edges

staple stem and leaf to back

let children decorate

Preparation: Fringe the edges of a paper plate with a scissors and fold back. Cut a stem and leaf (one piece) out of green construction paper and staple it behind the plate.
Activity: Children glue colored paper scraps into the centers of their flower heads.

MY WADING POOL

Materials: Paper plate, scissors, styrofoam meat tray, blue paint, sponge, snap clothespin.
Preparation: Pour blue paint in the styrofoam tray. Clip a clothespin onto a small sponge.
Activity: Children sponge paint blue water on their paper plate pools.

SHADE TREE

Materials: Brown wrapping paper or paper bag, scissors, shell macaroni, zip-lock bag, rubbing alcohol, green food coloring, paper towel, glue.
Preparation: Cut a large tree shape out of the brown paper. Place macaroni in the zip-lock bag, pour in alcohol and a little food coloring, then shake until all the macaroni is green. Remove the shells and let them dry on a paper towel.
Activity: Children glue macaroni leaves on their trees.

BACKYARD COLLAGE

Materials: Natural materials collected from the yard, styrofoam meat tray (a colored one, if possible), glue.
Preparation: Take the children on a nature walk in the backyard. Collect leaves, sticks, flowers, pine cones, grass, and the like.
Activity: Children glue the materials they have collected on a styrofoam tray to make a collage.

FLOWERS GROWING IN A ROW

Materials: Construction paper (including green), scissors, cupcake liners, glue, green marker.
Preparation: Cut out a strip of green construction paper and fringe it with scissors for grass. Also cut leaves out of the green paper.
Activity: First children glue a row of cupcake liners across the top of a full sheet of construction paper. Draw stem lines extending from these flower heads (some two-year-olds may be able to do this themselves). Next the children paste leaves on the stems, then a strip of grass at the base of the stems.

materials from the yard for the collage

SPONGE FLOWERS

Materials: Sponge, snap scissors, clothespin, styrofoam meat tray, paint, construction paper.
Preparation: Cut a flower shape out of the sponge. Clip a clothespin on back. Pour paint in the tray.
Activity: Children sponge paint flowers on paper.

MUSIC AND MOVEMENT ACTIVITIES

BUZZING BEES

The children pretend to be bees and flowers. The flowers blow about in the breeze. The bees make buzzing sounds as they chase the flowers, trying to land on them (by giving the flowers a hug).

LAWN MOWERS

Children hold hoops with both hands in front of themselves and push the hoops along the floor. As they mow, they make motor sounds.

HOW DOES YOUR GARDEN GROW?

Children perform a garden pantomime. Make the following suggestions: "First dig with a shovel (*stamp foot*), then rake (*comb floor with fingers*) and hoe (*chop at floor*). Next plant seeds (*pretend to drop seeds, then cover with soil and pat down*). Water the seeds every day (*pretend to pour watering can*)."

SPRINKLER FUN

Stand in the middle of a room or outdoors and pretend to be a lawn sprinkler. Swing your arms around as you call, "I'm a sprinkler and I'm getting you all wet!" The children run around you, pretending to get wet. They shake water off their bodies and stick out their tongues to get a drink. Tell them, "The ground is getting slippery! Everybody slip and fall! Now let's see you splash around in the puddle of water around the sprinkler."

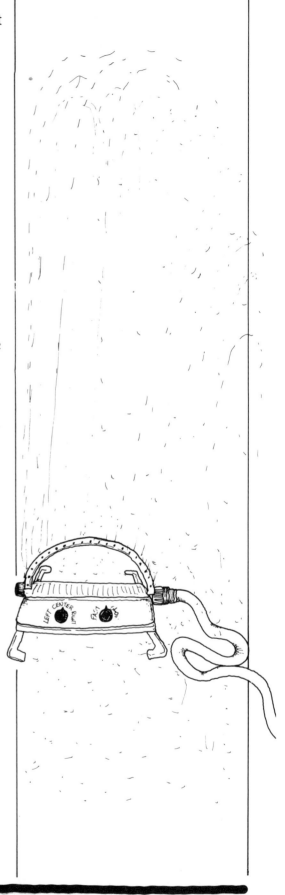

THE PARK

Going up in the air on a swing for the first time is a thrilling experience for young children—and the adult pushing has the pleasure of watching their pure joy. Some adventurous toddlers and two-year-olds will overcome their trepidations to climb the steps of a slide and take the flight down; others need rescuing at the top. Whether you live in a city or small town, playing in the park stimulates a lot of social interaction between you and your children.

ART ACTIVITIES

SWING MOBILE

Materials: Wire coat hanger, yarn or string, oaktag, scissors, hole punch, sponge, snap clothespin, styrofoam meat tray, paint.
Preparation: Cut a large toddler swing out of the oaktag. Punch a hole at the top on each side. Tie two short lengths of string or yarn (about 6 inches) onto the wire hanger. Pour paint in the styrofoam tray. Clip a clothespin on a piece of sponge.
Activity: Children sponge paint their toddler swings. When the paint has dried, tie the ends of the strings that are already attached to the hanger through the holes in the swing.

SHINY SLIDE

Materials: Construction paper, scissors, aluminum foil, glue.
Preparation: Cut a sliding board out of construction paper. Cut aluminum foil into small pieces.
Activity: Children glue the pieces of foil on their slides.

SILVER SEESAW

Materials: Oaktag, scissors, brass fastener, water-soluble school glue, paintbrush, silver glitter.
Preparation: Cut a large rectangle and a triangle out of the oaktag. Attach the triangle to the rectangle with a brass fastener as shown.
Activity: Children paint with glue on their seesaws, then sprinkle glitter on top. Shake off the excess glitter.

have children sponge paint their toddler swings

attach brass fastener

MUSIC AND MOVEMENT ACTIVITIES

SWINGING

Hold each child, then give the child a gentle push. The child runs forward, then back to you, then you push again. Younger children can sway from side to side after you push, or simply swing their arms up and down in a parallel motion.

ROUND ON THE MERRY-GO-ROUND

Hold hands and move in a circle as you sing this song to the tune of "Here We Go Round the Mulberry Bush."

> Here we go round on the merry-go-round
> The merry-go-round, the merry-go-round
> Here we go round on the merry-go-round
> Until it makes us dizzy.

Children stop moving to sing the second verse. Repeat for each child's name.

> The merry-go-round stops for Jessica, Jessica, Jessica.
> The merry-go-round stops for Jessica
> So she can climb on, too.

For the last verse, the children slow down, then sit.

> The merry-go-round closes down
> Closes down, closes down.
> The merry-go-round closes down
> We all go home and sleep.

SLIDING DOWN

Children pretend to go up and down a slide according to your suggestions. "Climb the steps to the top. (*Children walk in place.*) Now you're on top. (*Children stand with arms stretched up high.*) Slide down!" (*Children fall to their knees, then put their heads down on the floor with their arms on top of their heads.*)

SEESAW

Children pretend to be seesaws. Call out directions for the seesaws to go up (*children stand up and raise their arms over their heads*) or go down (*children squat*).

THE SUPERMARKET

A trip to the supermarket sparks the curiosity of young children. They survey the aisles of the store with anticipation; they know that what goes into the shopping cart turns up on the table at mealtime.

Name, classify, and count items with your child as you go down the aisles. Turn a chore into an opportunity for reinforcing language and concepts.

ART ACTIVITIES

STACKING CANS

Materials: Empty food cans of different sizes, materials for decorating (fabric scraps, macaroni, sequins, yarn, and the like), glue.
Preparation: Wash the cans and remove the labels.
Activity: Children decorate their cans by gluing on the various materials. When the glue has dried, the children stack the cans from largest to smallest.

SHOPPING CART

Materials: Construction paper, scissors, glue, paintbrush, silver glitter.
Preparation: Cut a shopping cart out of construction paper.
Activity: Children paint glue on their shopping carts, then sprinkle on glitter. Shake off the excess glitter.

BAG OF GROCERIES

Materials: Brown grocery bag, old magazines, scissors, glue.
Preparation: Cut out pictures of food from magazines.
Activity: Children fill their bags with groceries by gluing on food pictures.

MONEY IN THE REGISTER

Materials: Oaktag, scissors, play money, glue, money stamps and stamp pad (optional).
Preparation: Cut a cash register out of oaktag.
Activity: Children glue play money on their registers. If you have money stamps, they can also stamp on their registers.

BOX SCULPTURE

Materials: Assortment of small boxes in different shapes, glue, jar of paint, paintbrush.
Activity: Children glue boxes together however they like. When the glue has dried, they paint their sculptures.

MUSIC AND MOVEMENT ACTIVITIES

ROLLING CANS

Show the children how a real can rolls on the floor. Now it's their turn. The children lie on their backs and roll around the floor like cans. Ask them to tell you what kinds of food are inside their cans.

DOWN THE AISLES

The children act out shopping at the supermarket. Set up aisles with tables and chairs. The children push imaginary carts up and down the aisles, acting out your suggestions: "Go down the frozen food aisle. Brrr! It's cold here! Go down the dairy aisle and pick up milk, eggs, and cheese. Go down the meat aisle. Don't forget a loaf of bread! Now go to the check-out counter. Take your food out of the cart. The cashier pushes the buttons on the cash register—ring, ring! Pay the cashier. Help put the groceries in a brown bag and back into the shopping cart. Push the cart outside and take your bag of groceries home."

SONG: "A-Shopping We Will Go"

Sing this song to the tune of "The Farmer in the Dell."

A-shopping we will go
A-shopping we will go
In the front of the shopping cart
A-shopping we will go.

Peter (a child's name) gets some milk
Peter gets some milk
In the front of the shopping cart
Peter gets some milk.

Sing more verses using other children's names and different supermarket items—eggs, apples, and so on.

BALL IN THE BAG

Lay a brown bag on the floor with the open end facing the children. They take turns trying to roll a small ball into the bag.

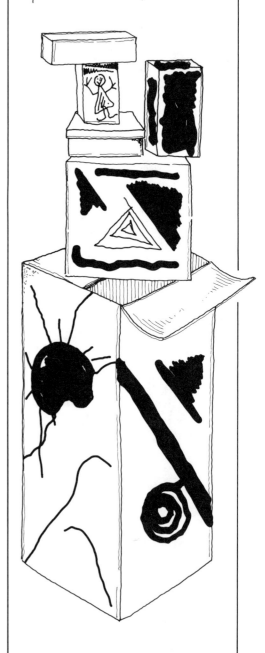

children glue their boxes together and then paint their sculptures

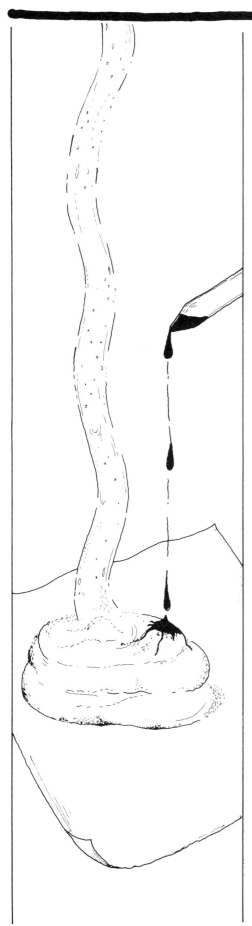

THE BEACH

Fresh air, sand, water—everybody enjoys a beach outing. Some toddlers and two-year-olds take to the water like little fish, while others are fearful. Give them time! Meanwhile, even the timid ones love to play with sand, and they're usually willing to venture far enough into the water to bring back a bucketful. That's not their only reward: As your children play with sand and water—mixing, pouring, sifting, and building—they pick up some readiness skills in the areas of language, math, and science.

ART ACTIVITIES

OCEAN WAVES

Materials: Finger paint paper or shelf paper, shaving cream, blue food coloring.
Preparation: Squirt shaving cream onto the paper. Drop blue food coloring on top of the shaving cream.
Activity: Children finger paint foamy blue waves with the shaving cream. *Note: Fingers will be blue for a while; the food coloring doesn't wash off.*

SHELL COLLAGE

Materials: Oaktag or heavy cardboard, small shells, glue.
Preparation: Take your children on a walk along the beach to collect a variety of shells. Wash the shells.
Activity: Children glue shells on oaktag or cardboard.

BEACH BALLS

Materials: Construction paper, scissors, black marker, sponge, snap clothespin, styrofoam meat tray, paint.
Preparation: Cut a large circle out of paper. Draw lines with the marker to show stripes on the beach ball. Clip a clothespin onto a small piece of sponge. Pour paint in the styrofoam tray.
Activity: Children sponge paint their balls.

STUFFED FISH

Materials: Brown wrapping paper, scissors, stapler, different-colored cellophane paper (available at craft supplies stores), glue, newspaper.
Preparation: Fold the brown paper in half and cut out two same-size fish. Staple the fish together, leaving an opening at

the tail. Cut the cellophane paper into small pieces. Shred the newspaper.

Activity: Children glue cellophane scales on both sides of the fish, then stuff the fish with shredded newspaper. Staple closed the tail.

SAND BUCKETS

Materials: Styrofoam cup, hole punch, pipe cleaner, shells, glue.
Preparation: Punch a hole on both sides of a styrofoam cup and attach a pipe cleaner for a handle.
Activity: Children glue shells around their buckets for decoration.

SHOVELS FULL OF SAND

Materials: Oaktag, scissors, aquarium sand, glue.
Preparation: Cut a shovel out of oaktag.
Activity: Children glue different colors of aquarium sand on their shovels.

MOVEMENT AND MUSIC

FLYING SEA GULLS

Children pretend to be sea gulls flying as you call out suggestions: "Flap your arms and fly high over the sea. Flap your arms and fly low by sitting on the floor. Fly to the sandy beach to look for food. Look—there's a piece of bread! Swoop down and pick it up with your beak, then eat it. Flap your arms again and fly away."

MAKING WAVES

You'll need a parachute or a large sheet. Everybody holds the parachute. Begin to shake it on the ground to make ripples. First shake slowly, then, as the imaginary wind picks up, shake faster. Now jump into the waves! (*Children go under the parachute.*) Swim! (*Children rotate arms to swim.*)

BEACH BALL BODY PARTS

Partners sit with their legs outstretched and roll a beach ball to one another. Next they stand up and throw the ball for one another to catch. Still in pairs, they try to hold the beach ball stomach to stomach, back to back, leg to leg, head to head. *Note: If a child has an adult for a partner, the adult will have to kneel.*

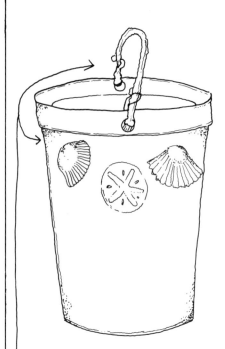

punch 2 holes in the top of cup and attach pipe cleaner

children go under blanket and rotate arms to swim

Chapter Four:

Animals I Like

TEDDY BEARS

What toddler has not cuddled up to a woolly teddy bear? Almost every child has one. Stories and activities about these familiar and lovable animals never fail to captivate young children. Yet teddy bears and other stuffed animals are more than simply objects of a child's affection. Children who talk to their animals and project their imaginary responses are practicing language and socialization.

ART ACTIVITIES

FEELS FURRY

Materials: Construction paper, scissors, fake fur scraps, felt scraps, velour scraps, glue.
Preparation: Cut a teddy bear shape out of construction paper.
Activity: Children glue fur and other soft materials on their teddy bears.

BEAR PUDDING

Materials: Instant chocolate pudding mix, bowl, measuring cup, milk, electric beater, spoon, washable surface (vinyl placemat, plastic tray, or formica table top).
Activity: Make chocolate pudding with the children. Drop a few spoonfuls on a washable surface and let the children finger paint with the bear-colored pudding, tasting as they paint.

BEAR'S TREE

Materials: Oaktag, scissors, twigs, acorns, bits of tree bark, glue.
Preparation: Cut the shape of a tree out of oaktag. Take the children on a scavenger hunt to find tree materials—twigs, bark, leaves, etc.
Activity: Children glue natural materials on their trees.

BEAR COLORS

Materials: Finger paint paper or shelf paper, brown and black fingerpaint.
Activity: Children finger paint, swirling bear colors on their papers.

cut out teddy bears and let children glue on fur

let children glue natural materials on their trees

let the children use the
sponge bears to make
wrapping paper

TEDDY BEAR, TEDDY BEAR

Materials: Brown wrapping paper or paper bag, scissors, styrofoam meat tray, paint, sponge, snap clothespin.
Preparation: Cut a teddy bear shape out of brown paper. Pour paint in the styrofoam tray. Clip a clothespin on a small piece of sponge.
Activity: Children sponge paint their bears. The rough impressions made by the sponge will look like a woolly bearskin.

PANDA BEAR

Materials: Black construction paper, scissors, white cotton balls or white fabric scraps, glue.
Preparation: Cut the shape of a panda bear out of the black paper. Cut white fabric scraps into small pieces.
Activity: Children glue white cotton or fabric patches on the panda bear's stomach, back and face.

BEAR GIFT WRAP

Materials: Brown wrapping paper or roll of newsprint, sponge, scissors, styrofoam meat tray, paint.
Preparation: Cut a teddy bear shape out of the sponge. Pour the paint in the styrofoam tray.
Activity: Children sponge paint bears on the wrapping paper or a generous piece of newsprint. The dry sheets can be used to wrap presents.

BEAR RUGS

Materials: Carpet samples or scraps (available for free or a minimal charge at carpet stores), utility knife, buttons, felt, glue.
Preparation: Use the utility knife to cut a simple bear shape out of the carpet. Cut circles out of felt for a muzzle and nose.
Activity: Children glue button eyes and felt muzzles and noses on their woolly carpet bears.

MUSIC AND MOVEMENT ACTIVITIES

WALK LIKE A BEAR

Show the children how a bear lumbers about on all fours. As the children move about the room, pounding their heavy arms and legs like huge bears, encourage them to growl like bears, too.

CLIMBING BEARS

Children pretend to be bears climbing a tree. They stand on tiptoes with arms and hands stretched overhead. They stretch one hand on top of the other with clenched fists. When they reach the top of the tree, they slide down by falling to the floor.

THROUGH THE FOREST

Make an obstacle course with blocks, a table, and chairs. Children pretend to be bears jumping over a big stone (a block), crawling through a cave (a table), and under some berry bushes (chairs).

FINGER PLAY: "I'm a Little Teddy Bear"

I'm a little teddy bear, teddy bear, teddy bear
(*Wiggle one thumb.*)
I'm a little teddy bear, I play with you.
(*Wiggle both thumbs.*)
I'm a little teddy bear, teddy bear, teddy bear
(*Wiggle one thumb.*)
I'm a little teddy bear, we sleep together, too!
(*One thumb lies on top of the other.*)
You're my little teddy bear, teddy bear, teddy bear
(*Wiggle one thumb.*)
You're my little teddy bear, shop with Mom and me.
(*Wiggle both thumbs and one index finger.*)
You're my little teddy bear, teddy bear, teddy bear
(*Wiggle one thumb.*)
You're my little teddy bear, in the car we go all three!
(*Wiggle both thumbs and one index finger.*)
Bye, bye! (*Wave hand.*)

BUNNY RABBITS

Young children encountering a bunny rabbit will first watch curiously, taking in the long floppy ears, twitching nose, and quick hops. Then they give chase, but the rabbit always manages to disappear into some small crevice. In some homes, the Easter Bunny is a little more obliging, leaving behind a basket of treats. The only rabbits toddlers may fear are the ones impersonating the Easter Bunny at shopping centers around holiday time. If your child is frightened by a beckoning bunny, move on. Next year the same child may be mature enough to enjoy a visit.

ART ACTIVITIES

RABBIT STENCIL

Materials: Oaktag, scissors, masking tape, construction paper, paint, paintbrush.
Preparation: Cut a rabbit shape out of the middle of a piece of oaktag. Tape the stencil onto the construction paper.
Activity: Children paint through the rabbit stencil to produce a bunny on their papers. Reposition the stencil to make more bunnies.

BUNNY EARS

Materials: Oaktag (preferably pink), scissors, stapler, cotton balls, glue.
Preparation: Cut out a strip of oaktag two inches wide and a little longer than the circumference of the child's head. Also cut out two ovals for ears and staple these in the center of the strip.
Activity: Children glue cotton balls on their bunny ears. Fit the hat strip around each child's head, remove, then staple the overlap. The children parade around the room wearing their bunny ears.

COTTONTAIL PAINTING

Materials: Construction paper, styrofoam meat tray, paint, cotton balls.
Preparation: Pour the paint in the styrofoam tray.
Activity: Children dab cotton balls in paint, then brush the paint on their papers.

have children make bunnies on their papers using the stencil

CARROT PRINTS

Materials: Construction paper, carrot, styrofoam meat tray, orange paint.
Preparation: Slice off the top of a carrot. Pour the paint in the styrofoam tray.
Activity: Children press the carrot top into the paint, then print with it on paper. They can snack on the unused part of the carrot.

RABBIT HUTCH

Materials: Actual rabbit hutch or a picture, fine wire screen about 6 inches square, tape 1½ inches wide, construction paper, styrofoam meat tray, paint, toothbrush.
Preparation: Fold the tape over the edges of the wire screen to make a frame.
Activity: Show the children the hutch or a picture of one. The children lay the screen on a piece of paper, then paint through it with the toothbrush. Remove the screen and admire the design.

COTTONTAIL

Materials: Oaktag, scissors, cotton balls, glue, masking tape.
Preparation: Cut an oval out of the oaktag.
Activity: Children glue cotton balls on the oval to make a bunny's fluffy tail. Attach the tails to the children's bottoms with masking tape.

MUSIC AND MOVEMENT ACTIVITIES

WIGGLING COTTONTAILS

You'll need the bunny ears and cottontails the children made in previous art activities. Help the children put on their ears and tails. The children pretend to be bunnies. First they squat with their tails touching the floor. They hop to a standing position, wiggle their tails, hop around the room some more, then find a place to crouch and hide.

If you have a recording of "The Bunny Hop," play it while the children hop about the room.

SONG: "Little Bunny"

Sing this song to the tune of "My Darling Clementine."

Little bunny, little bunny
Little bunny I love you.
You are soft and warm and furry.
Play with me the whole day through.

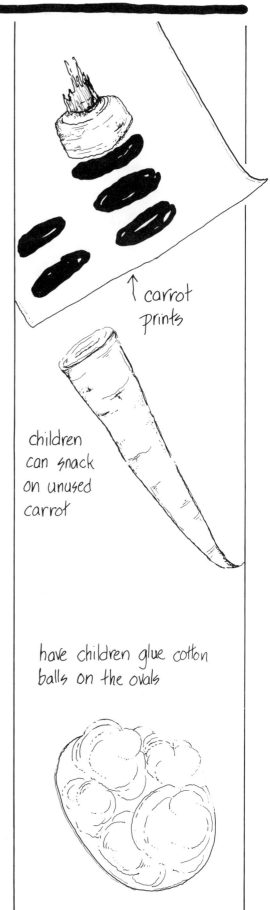

carrot prints

children can snack on unused carrot

have children glue cotton balls on the ovals

DOGS AND PUPPIES

Most young children have had direct experiences with dogs—their own pet, or a friend's or neighbor's pet. A dog's size or cries will leave a lasting impression on a toddler or two-year-old, sometimes evoking love, sometimes uncertainty or fear. Your own response to an encounter with a dog or other domesticated animal will often signal the children's response, so for their sake hide any fears as best you can. If possible, give your children a stuffed dog to play with before they meet the real thing.

ART ACTIVITIES

A BONE FOR MY DOG

Materials: Oaktag, scissors, small dog bones and multi-colored dog treats (both available in supermarkets), glue.
Preparation: Cut a large dog bone out of oaktag.
Activity: Children glue real bones and treats on the oaktag bone. *Note: Caution the children not to eat the dog treats. They're good for dogs, not children.*

DOG HOUSE

Materials: Oaktag, scissors, old magazines, wood scraps (ask for them at a lumber yard or hardware store), wood shavings (for a hamster or gerbil cage, available at pet stores), glue.
Preparation: Cut a dog house out of oaktag. Draw in the doorway. Cut a picture of a dog out of a magazine.
Activity: Children first glue the picture of the dog in the doorway of the dog house, then glue wood scraps and shavings on the rest of the house.

DROOPY EARS

Materials: Two paper plates, scissors, stapler, yarn (one color), glue, bottle caps or buttons, pipe cleaners.
Preparation: Cut two ovals for ears out of one paper plate and staple them onto another paper plate to make the dog's head. Snip the yarn into small pieces.
Activity: Children glue yarn snippets on the paper plate dog. Help the children glue on caps or buttons for eyes and a nose, and pipe cleaners for a mouth and whiskers.

use pipe cleaners for whiskers and mouth, use buttons for eyes and nose

DOG BED

Materials: Finger paint paper or shelf paper, scissors, brown construction paper, fingerpaint, spoon, glue.
Preparation: Cut an oval-shaped dog bed out of the finger-paint paper or shelf paper. Cut a dog out of construction paper to fit in the dog bed. Spoon some finger paint onto the bed cutout.
Activity: Children finger paint the dog bed. When the paint has dried, they glue a dog on the bed.

BONE PRINTS

Materials: Hollow dog bone with a flat end, construction paper, styrofoam meat tray, brown paint.
Preparation: Pour the paint into the styrofoam tray.
Activity: Children make bone prints by pressing the end of the bone into the paint, then onto the paper.

COLLAR, TAG, AND LEASH

Materials: Oaktag, scissors, colored construction paper, pen or marker, decorations (such as leather scraps, bells, glitter, and sequins), glue, stapler, hole punch, shoelace.
Preparation: Cut out a strip of oaktag for a dog collar. Also cut out a small construction paper circle for a dog tag.
Activity: Children glue the dog tag in the center of the dog collar, then glue decorations on the dog collar. Write the name of a real or imaginary pet on the dog tag. When the glue has dried, overlap and staple together the two ends of the oaktag strip to form the collar. Punch a hole in the collar opposite the dog tag and tie on the shoelace for a leash.

MUSIC AND MOVEMENT ACTIVITIES

BEANBAG BONES

One child throws a beanbag, pretending it's a dog bone. Another child gets down on hands and knees, pretending to be a dog, and runs (crawls) to retrieve the beanbag bone. The children switch roles.

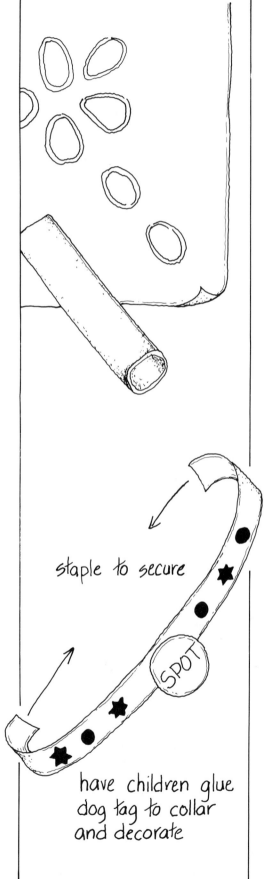

staple to secure

have children glue dog tag to collar and decorate

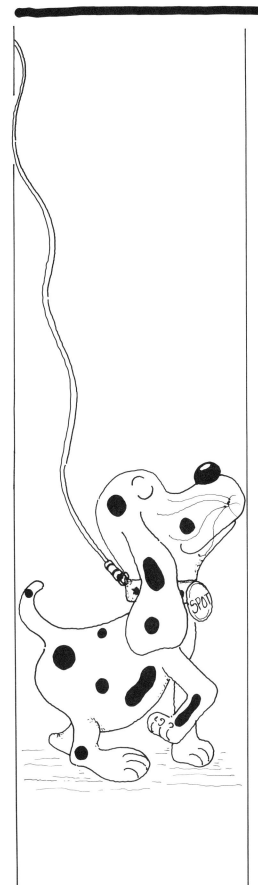

SONG: "Where Has My Little Dog Gone?"

The children sing this song as they pretend to search about with their hands to their foreheads in a conventional seeking gesture.

> Oh where, oh where has my little dog gone?
> Oh where, oh where can he be?
> With his ears cut short and his tail cut long,
> Oh where, oh where is he?

WALKING MY DOG

Two children perform together as you narrate. Each child holds one end of a rope. One child is the dog walker; the other is the dog. The dog walker walks slowly and the rope is slack as the dog leads, sniffing about. The dog picks up its pace; so does the dog walker. Suddenly the dog sees a cat and starts to pull on the rope. The dog is off chasing, dragging the dog walker, who must also run. The cat runs up a tree, so the dog slows and stops. The walker also slows and stops. Then the dog and dog walker head back home.

WAGGING MY TAIL

Children hold yarn hair ribbons or crepe paper streamers behind their backs and pretend to be dogs wagging their tails back and forth. They walk, run, and jump as they wag their tails.

DOGS DIGGING

Children pretend to be dogs digging holes. First they scratch the surface of the ground, then dig deeper and deeper, dirt flying all around them. The hole gets bigger and bigger (*dig a wider space*). Finally the dog runs to the side, gets its bone, brings it back to the hole and drops it in. Then the dog kicks dirt back in the hole. The bone is buried!

CATS AND KITTENS

A toddler's energy is boundless—almost as boundless as a kitten's, which may be why small children are so attracted to them. Even a grown-up cat stays reassuringly small, so with the exception of its claws, a cat is no threat to a toddler. On the other hand, cats and kittens may need your protection from the terrors of a two-year-old tail chaser. Like bears, bunnies, and dogs, cats are often a part of your child's stuffed menagerie, so the first encounter can be through play.

ART ACTIVITIES

PAW PRINTS

Materials: Sponge, scissors, construction paper, styrofoam meat tray, paint.
Preparation: Cut a cat's paw out of the sponge. Pour paint in the styrofoam tray.
Activity: Children press the sponge paw in the paint, then print with it on paper.

BALL OF YARN

Materials: Construction paper, scissors, assorted colored yarn, glue.
Preparation: Cut a large circle out of construction paper. Snip the yarn into small pieces, from one to three inches long.
Activity: Children glue the snippets of yarn on their paper balls.

BOWL OF MILK

Materials: Construction paper, scissors, empty roll-on deodorant bottle, white paint.
Preparation: Cut a bowl out of construction paper. Pry out the bubble in the deodorant bottle and pour in white paint, then snap the bubble back in.
Activity: Children roll the paint bottle on the bowl to fill it with "milk."

cut cat's paw out of sponge

have children glue yarn to circles

glue tube to cardboard and have children glue carpet squares to tube

wrap fur scrap around glued tube

glue decorated cat face to tube

FURRY KITTY

Materials: Oaktag, scissors, felt marker or buttons and yarn, empty toilet tube, fur scrap (from furrier or fabric store), glue.
Preparation: Cut a cat face out of oaktag. Draw cat features if the children are not able to glue them on.
Activity: Children put glue all around the toilet tube and wrap the fur scrap around it. They glue button eyes and nose and yarn whiskers on the cat face. Then they glue the face on one open end of the tube.

CAT FOOD COLLAGE

Materials: Dry cat food (different shapes and sizes, if possible), construction paper, glue.
Activity: Children glue pieces of dry cat food on paper to make a collage. *Note: Caution the children not to eat the cat food.*

SCRATCHING POST

Materials: Empty paper towel tube, three-inch square of cardboard, carpet scraps, glue.
Preparation: Glue the towel tube upright on the cardboard square. Cut the carpet scraps into square-inch pieces.
Activity: Children glue carpet scraps on the towel tube.

SOFT AS A KITTEN

Materials: Construction paper, scissors, colored markers, glue, cotton balls, soft-textured fabric scraps (fake fur, velvet, velour), yarn.
Preparation: Cut a cat out of construction paper.
Activity: Children glue materials that are "as soft as a kitten" on their paper cats.

MUSIC AND MOVEMENT ACTIVITIES

BALL OF YARN

You'll need a yard of yarn rolled into a ball for each child. Children pretend to be playful kittens with a ball of yarn. They hold one end and run around the room as the ball unravels. They continue to run, pulling along the yarn, until you signal them to stop. Tie all the pieces of yarn together to form a circle. Ask the children to sit by their own piece of yarn in the circle and purr like contented cats.

SONG: "Old Gray Cat"

The children sing and act out the verses, some playing the cat and some the mice.

The old gray cat is sleeping, sleeping, sleeping
The old gray cat is sleeping in the house.
(*Children pretend to sleep.*)
The little mice are eating, eating, eating
The little mice are eating in the house.
(*Children nibble fingers.*)
The old gray cat goes creeping, creeping, creeping
The old gray cat goes creeping in the house.
(*Children crawl very slowly.*)
The little mice go scampering, scampering, scampering
The little mice go scampering in the house.
(*Children crawl very quickly.*)

AWAKE AND STRETCH

Children move like cats. They get on their hands and knees. They round their backs, then straighten them. They repeat, saying "Meow, meow!" Then they reach with their arms and swat at something, saying "Hiss, hiss!" They crawl around again on all fours, then rest their faces on their hands as they pretend to nap, purring like contented cats.

HUNGRY CATS

Children pretend to be cats crying for food. They get on all fours and meow at you. Pour some imaginary milk in a bowl. The cats move their tongues in and out as they pretend to drink. Then they clean themselves, pretending to lick their paws and bodies.

LITTLE PUSSY CAT

Have the children recite and act out this nursery rhyme.

Who's that ringing our front door bell?
(*Children pretend to push a door bell.*)
I'm a little pussy cat and I'm not very well.
(*Children on all fours pretending to cry.*)
Then put your nose in a little mutton fat.
(*Children rub their noses.*)
And that's the way to cure a little pussy cat.
(*Children on all fours meow.*)

READ-ALOUD BOOKS FOR TODDLERS AND TWO-YEAR-OLDS

Reading aloud to your children is the best way to introduce and supplement the activities in each unit of this book. Pages 61-64 list appropriate titles on every theme for both age groups—toddlers and two-year-olds. However, the age designations are not hard and fast. You are the best judge of what kind of material your children can understand and appreciate. Read a book through yourself, then decide whether or not it's for your particular child or group of children.

Chapter One: All About Me
MY BODY

Read-aloud books for toddlers
Goldsborough. June. *Look at Me*. Western, 1982.
Kilroy, Sally. *Babies' Bodies*. Four Winds Press, 1983.
Tymms, Jean. *My Head-to-Toe Book*. Western, 1974.
——————— . *All By Myself*. Price/Stern/Sloan, 1979.

Read-aloud books for two-year-olds
Brenner, Barbara. *Faces*. E. P. Dutton, 1970.
Bruna, Dick. *When I'm Big*. Price/Stern/Sloan, 1984.
——————— . *Lisa and Lynn*. Price/Stern/Sloan, 1984.
Goldsborough, June. *I Can Do It By Myself*. Western, 1981.
Holzenthaler, Jean. *My Hands Can*. E. P. Dutton, 1979.
——————— . *My Feet Do*. E. P. Dutton, 1979.
LeSieg, Theo. *The Eye Book*. Random House, 1968.
Wolde, Gunilla. *Betsy and Peter Are Different*. Random House, 1982.

MY CLOTHING

Read-aloud books for toddlers
Baird, Anne. *Baby Socks*. William Morrow, 1984.
McCue, Dick. *Teddy Dresses*. Simon and Schuster, 1983.
Oxenbury, Helen. *Dressing*. Simon and Schuster, 1981.
Peek, Merle. *Mary Wore Her Red Dress*. Clarion, 1985.
Swan, Susan. *Button Gets Dressed*. Modern Promotion Publishers, 1984.
Szekeres, Cyndy. *Thumpity, Thump Gets Dressed*. Western, 1984.

Watanabe, Shigeo. *How Do I Put It On?* Putnam, 1977.
Wells, Rosemary. *Max's New Suit*. Dial, 1979.
Ziefert, Harriet. *Zippety, Zip!* Viking, 1984.

Read-aloud books for two-year-olds
Bruna, Dick. *I Can Dress Myself*. Methuen, 1978.
——————— . *My Shirt Is White*. Methuen, 1972.
James, Diane. *My Clothes*. Ray Rourke, 1981.
Lloyd, David. *Boots*. Simon and Schuster, 1983.

MY FAMILY AND FRIENDS
Read-aloud books for toddlers
Oexbury, Helen. *Mother's Helper*. Dial, 1982.
——————— . *Family*. Simon and Schuster, 1981.
Wantanabe, Shiego. *Where's My Daddy?* Philomel, 1982.
——————— . *All Together*. Price/Stern/Sloan, 1963.

Read-aloud books for two-year-olds
Asch, Frank. *Just Like Daddy*. Prentice-Hall, 1981.
Burningham, John. *The Baby*. Crowell, 1976.
Fujikawa, Gyo. *Babies*. Grosset and Dunlap, 1963.
Kenworthy, Catherine. *I Like to Help My Mommy*. Western, 1981.
Manley, Deborah. *Our Baby*. Ray Rourke, 1981.
Wolde, Gunilla. *Betsy's Baby Brother*. Random House, 1975.

MY HOME
Read-aloud books for toddlers
Hill, Eric. *At Home*. Random, 1983.
Johnson, John E. *This Is My House*. Western, 1981.
Lindgren, Barbro. *Sam's Lamp*. William Morrow, 1983.
Maestro, Betsy and Giulio. *Harriet at Home*. Crown, 1983.
Tarsky, Sue. *Table and Chair*. Simon and Schuster, 1983.
Zokeisha. *Doll House*. Simon and Schuster, 1984.
——————— . *Listen to That*. Western, 1980.
——————— . *My House*. Western, 1978.
——————— . *A First Book in My Kitchen*. Brimax Books, England, 1980.
——————— . *In the House*. Price/Stern/Sloan, 1979.

Read-aloud books for two-year-olds
Barton, Byron. *Building a House*. Greenwillow, 1981.
Burningham, John. *The Cupboard*. Crowell, 1975.
Krauss, Ruth. *A Very Special House*. Harper and Row, 1953.
McNoughton, Colin. *At Home*. Philomel, 1982.

Rockwell, Harlow. *My Kitchen.* Greenwillow, 1980.

Virin, Anna. *Elsa Tidies Her House.* Harvey House, 1978.

Wolde, Gunilla. *Betsy and the Vacuum Cleaner.* Random House, 1982.

Chapter Two: My Day at Home
MY MEALS
Read-aloud books for toddlers
Bertrand, Micheline and Marin, Lise. *Cuddles' Mealtime.* Brimax Books, England, 1984.

Lindgren, Barbro. *Sam's Cookie.* William Morrow, 1983.

Lloyd, David. *Bread and Cheese.* Random House, 1984.

Tarsky, Sue. *Apple and Pear.* Simon and Schuster, 1983.

Watanabe, Shigeo. *What a Good Lunch!* Philomel, 1978.

Wells, Rosemary. *Max's Breakfast.* Dial, 1985.

Ziefert, Harriet. *Munchety, Munch!* Viking, 1984.

——————— . *Mealtime.* Price/Stern/Sloan, 1981.

——————— . *At the Table.* Price/Stern/Sloan, 1981.

Read-aloud books for two-year-olds
Black, Irma Simonton. *Is This My Dinner?* Albert Whitman, 1972.

Bruna, Dick. *The Apple.* Price/Stern/Sloan, 1981.

Burningham, John. *The Cupboard.* Crowell, 1975.

Fujikawa, Gyo. *Let's Eat.* Grossett and Dunlap, 1975.

Lloyd, David. *Bread and Cheese.* Random, 1975.

Oxenbury, Helen. *Eating Out.* Dial Books, 1983.

MY BATH AND POTTY
Read-aloud books for toddlers
Allison, Alida. *The Toddler's Potty Book.* Price/Stern/Sloan, 1979.

Bertrand, Micheline and Marin, Lise. *Cuddles' Bathtime.* Brimax Books, England, 1984.

Lindgren, Barbro. *Sam's Bath.* William Morrow, 1983.

Swan, Susan. *Button Takes a Bath.* Modern Promotion Publishers, 1984.

Wells, Rosemary. *Max's Bath.* Dial, 1985.

——————— . *Bathtime.* Price/Stern/Sloan, 1981.

Read-aloud books for two-year-olds
Barrett, Judi. *I Hate to Take a Bath.* Modern Promotion Publishers, 1984.

Brooks, Joae G. *No More Diapers!* Delacorte, 1984.

Frankel, Alona. *Once Upon a Potty.* Barron's Educational Series, 1984.

Lloyd, David. *Bathtime.* Simon and Schuster, 1983.

Mack, Alison. *Toilet Learning: The Picture Book Technique for Children and Parents.* Little, Brown, 1978.

MY NAP AND BEDTIME
Read-aloud books for toddlers
Bertrand, Micheline and Marin, Lise. *Cuddles' Bedtime.* Brimax Books, England, 1984.

Boynton, Sandra. *The Going to Bed Book.* Simon and Shuster, 1982.

Kozikowski, Renate. *Titus Bear Goes to Bed.* Harper and Row, 1984.

Oxenbury, Helen. *Good Night, Good Morning.* Dial, 1982.

Wells, Rosemary. *Max's Bedtime.* Dial, 1985.

Wilkin, Eloise. *Baby's Bedtime.* Grosset and Dunlap, 1985.

——————— . *Bedtime.* Price/Stern/Sloan, 1981.

Read-aloud books for two-year-olds
Brown, Margaret Wise. *A Child's Good Night Book.* Addison-Wesley, 1943.

——————— . *Goodnight Moon.* Harper and Row, 1947.

Burningham, John. *The Blanket.* Crowell, 1975.

Burrowes, Elizabeth. *A Sleepy Story.* Western, 1982.

Chalmers, Mary. *Take a Nap, Harry.* Harper and Row, 1981.

Chorao, Kay. *Kate's Quilt.* E. P. Dutton, 1975.

Fujikawa, Gyo. *Sleepytime.* Grosset and Dunlap, 1981.

Wilkink, Eloise. *My Goodnight Book.* Western, 1981.

MY TOYS
Read-aloud books for toddlers
Bertrand, Micheline and Marin, Lise. *Cuddles' Playtime.* Brimax Books, England, 1984.

Hargreaves, Roger. *Mr. Tickle's Toys.* Price/Stern/Sloan, 1981.

Oxenbury, Helen. *Playing.* Simon and Schuster, 1981.

Swan, Susan. *Playtime for Button.* Modern Promotion Publishers, 1982.

Tarsky, Sue. *Doll and Drum.* Simon and Schuster, 1983.

——————— . *Playtime.* Simon and Schuster, 1983.

Wells, Rosemary. *Max's Toys.* Dial, 1979.

Wilkin, Eloise. *Baby's Toys.* Grosset and Dunlap, 1985.

Ziefert, Harriet. *Diggety, Dig!* Viking, 1984.
_____ . *Baby's First Toys*. Platt and Munk, 1972.
_____ . *Playtime*. Price/Stern/Sloan, 1981.
_____ . *Things I Like to Play With*. Simon and Schuster, 1981.

Read-aloud books for two-year-olds
Bruna, Dick. *Miffy at the Playground*. Price/Stern/Sloan, 1984.
Burningham, John. *The Friend*. Crowell, 1976.
Chorao, Kay. *Kate's Box*. E. P. Dutton, 1982.
Ets, Marie Hall. *Play With Me*. Western, 1968.
Fujikawa, Gyo. *Let's Play*. Grosset and Dunlap, 1975.
Lloyd, David. *Ball*. Simon and Schuster, 1983
Maestro, Betsy and Giulio. *Harriet at Play*. Crown, 1984.
Manley, Deborah. *My Work*. Ray Rourke, 1981.
Mayer, Mercer. *Play With Me*. Western, 1982.
Peppe, Rodney. *Games*. Viking, 1983.
_____ . *Little Dolls*. Viking, 1983.

Chapter Three: When I'm Out

MY YARD

Read-aloud books for toddlers
Seiden, Art. *Look on the Ground*. Grosset and Dunlap, 1982.
_____ . *Look in the Yard*. Grosset and Dunlap, 1982.
Swan, Susan. *Button's Garden*. Modern Promotional Publishers, 1984.

Read-aloud books for two-year-olds
Fujikawa, Gyo. *Let's Grow a Garden*. Grosset and Dunlap, 1978.
Kraus, Ruth. *The Carrot Seed*. Harper and Row, 1954.
Rockwell, Anne and Harlow. *My Back Yard*. Macmillan, 1984.
Undry. *A Tree Is Nice*. Harper and Row, 1956.

THE PARK

Read-aloud books for toddlers
McNaughton, Colin. *At the Park*. Philomel, 1982.
Watanabe, Shigeo. *I'm the King of the Castle!* Philomel, 1982.
Wilkin, Eloise. *Baby's Playground*. Grosset and Dunlap, 1985.

Read-aloud books for two-year-olds
Bruna, Dick. *Miffy at the Playground*. Price/Stern/Sloan, 1984.
Schroeder, Binette. *Tuffa and the Picnic*. Dial, 1983.
Virin, Anna. *Elsa's Bears in the Playground*. Harvey House, 1978.

THE SUPERMARKET

Read-aloud books for toddlers
McNaughton, Colin. *At the Stores*. Philomel, 1982.
Oxenbury, Helen. *Shopping Trip*. Dial, 1981.
Tarsky, Sue. *Shopping*. Simon and Schuster, 1983.

Read-aloud books for two-year-olds
Burningham, John. *The Shopping Basket*. Crowell, 1982.
Rockwell, Anne and Harlow. *The Supermarket*. Macmillan, 1979.
Spier, Peter. *Food Market*. Doubleday, 1981.

THE BEACH

Read-aloud books for toddlers and twos
Bruna, Dick. *Miffy at the Seashore*. Price/Stern/Sloan, 1984.
Kozikowski, Renate. *Titus Bear Goes to the Beach*. Harper and Row, 1984.
Oxenbury, Helen. *Beach Day*. Dial, 1982.

Chapter Four: Animals I Like

TEDDY BEARS

Read-aloud books for toddlers
Bracken, Carolyn. *The Little Teddy Bear*. Simon and Schuster, 1982.
Hill, Eric. *Good Morning Baby Bear*. Random House, 1984.
Lindgren, Barbro. *Sam's Lamp*. William Morrow, 1983.
Ono, Koichi. *The Panda Bear*. Simon and Schuster, 1982.
_____ . *Busy Bear*. Western, 1980.
_____ . *Panda*. Brimax Books, England, 1983.
_____ . *Teddy*. Brimax Books, England, 1983.

Read-aloud books for two-year-olds
Asch, Frank. *Moon Bear*. Scribner, 1978.
Cavley, Lorinda Bryan. *Goldilocks and the Three Bears*. Putnam, 1981.
Flack, Marjorie. *Ask Mr. Bear*. Macmillan, 1966.
Fujikawa, Gyo. *Betty Bear's Birthday*. Grosset and Dunlap, 1975.
Kraus, Robert. *Milton the Early Riser*. Simon and Schuster, 1972.
Nakatani. *My Teddy Bear*. Crowell, 1976.
Pfloog, Jan. *The Bear Book*. Western, 1965.
Savage, Kathleen and Siewert, Margaret. *Bear Hunt*. Prentice-Hall, 1976.
Struyck, Hanneke. *Bobby Bear*. Baron's Educational Series, 1984.
Szekeres, Cyndy. *Baby Bear's Surprise*. Western, 1984.
Virin, Anna. *Elsa's Bears*. Harvey House, 1978.

BUNNY RABBITS

Read-aloud books for toddlers

Hands, Hargrave. *Bunny Sees*. Grosset and Dunlap, 1985.

Scarry, Richard. *I Am a Bunny*. Western, 1963.

——————— . *Rabbit*. Brimax Books, England, 1983.

Read-aloud books for two-year-olds

Becker, John. *Seven Little Rabbits*. Scholastic, 1976.

Burningham, John. *The Rabbit*. Crowell, 1976.

Hoban, Tana. *Where Is It?* Macmillan, 1974.

Kraus, Robert. *The Littlest Rabbit*. Scholastic, 1961.

Struyck, Hanneke. *Helen Hare*. Baron's Educational Series, 1984.

Szerkeres, Cyndy. *Thumpity Thump Gets Dressed*. Western, 1984.

PUPPIES AND DOGS

Read-aloud books for toddlers

Chandoha, Walter. *Puppies and Kittens*. Platt and Munk, 1983.

Hands, Hargrave. *Puppy Sees*. Grosset and Dunlap, 1985.

Schroeder, Binette. *Tuffa and the Bone*. Dial, 1983.

Szekeres, Cyndy. *Puppy Too Small*. Western, 1984.

Read-aloud books for two-year-olds

Burningham, John. *The Dog*. Crowell, 1976.

Hill, Eric. *Where's Spot?* Putnam, 1980.

Oxenbury, Helen. *Our Dog*. Dial, 1984.

Pfloog, Jan. *Puppies Are Like That*. Random House, 1975.

Risom, Ole. *I Am a Puppy*. Western, 1970.

——————— . *Puppies*. Western, 1982.

KITTENS AND CATS

Read-aloud books for toddlers

Chandoha, Walter. *Puppies and Kittens*. Platt and Munk, 1983.

Pfloog, Jan. *Kittens*. Random House, 1977.

Schongut, Emanuel. *Look Kitten*. Simon and Schuster, 1983. Also *Play Kitten*, *Wake Kitten*, *Hush Kitten*, and *Catch Kitten*.

Szekeres, Cyndy. *Scaredy Cat*. Western, 1984.

Read-aloud books for two-year-olds

Polushkin. *Who Said Meow?* Crown, 1975.

Risom, Ole. *I Am a Kitten*. Western, 1970.

Rubel, Nicole. *Me and My Kitty*. Macmillan, 1983.

——————— . *Kittens*. Western, 1982.